Delinquent Conduct and Broken Homes

DELINQUENT CONDUCT

AND

BROKEN HOMES

A Study of 1,050 Boys

RICHARD S. STERNE

COLLEGE & UNIVERSITY PRESS · *Publishers*

NEW HAVEN, CONN.

MANUFACTURED IN THE UNITED STATES OF AMERICA BY
UNITED PRINTING SERVICES, INC.
NEW HAVEN, CONN.

TO MY FAMILY

FOREWORD

Many hypotheses have been advanced in the search for explanations of delinquent behavior. Some rest on common-sense observation, others on the findings of formal studies. Their factual basis has often been questionable due to the paucity of data. Other studies have frequently been deficient because of the absence of an adequate theoretical framework governing the selection and the analysis of data. In either case, their conclusions have often been accepted and cited — without proper corroboration, and where the evidence has been contradictory attempts to settle the issues have often not been made. Among the hypotheses a number refer to the institution of the family and its influence on the delinquency of its members. The family's internal moral climate, its milieu, its economic or class status, its composition, its stability, and other of its characteristics have been investigated with this in mind. A great many investigations have touched directly or peripherally upon the effect of broken homes on the conduct of children raised in them. In focusing his attention on this specific problem, the author has produced a study which helps to clarify it and is therefore a worthy addition to the literature of criminological research.

THORSTEN SELLIN

PREFACE

In a certain city there is a ramshackle house in which two families live. The wives are sisters. One husband is a mechanic; the other, an unskilled laborer from Oklahoma and father of two girls and a boy of five years.

The second couple do not get along well. The mother-in-law is often in the house tyrannizing both sisters' children and interfering in their family life, while posing as a baby-sitter. She has become a source of bitter conflict. One day the husband and wife have a terrible quarrel over her. They shriek and scream. The children are terrified. The father yells that he is leaving home for Oklahoma and is never coming back. He storms out the front door and shouts that any kids who want to go with him had better come now. The small boy is torn by his loyalties. He falteringly follows the father. He gets into his father's car. A few minutes later, it roars back into the yard and the boy runs up the walk to his mother. The car roars away.

After a year, the mother obtains a divorce on grounds of desertion. She takes up with a filling station owner twice her age for whom she works as a bookkeeper. They marry. He joins the woman and her three children in the house with her sister, mechanic husband, and their children.

The two men take a tolerant interest in the youngster. His uncle smilingly says that he lets the children play in his workshop, even though they always lose his tools. The young boy, now seven, has a broken home. He has been deserted. His parents have been divorced. He has a stepfather.

Is this boy more likely to become a delinquent than if these things had not happened? Are his chances of being a good citizen fewer than they would have been under happier circumstances?

One boy's story has been told, and there are many, many like him, with the same or similar problems. What of their future development and their potential for delinquency? The exigencies of these children have raised a controversy which through years of debate has reached no conclusion. Does a break in the family crucially affect the social control of juveniles? Does the type of break matter?—suppose the boy had lost his father through death and not such terrible turmoil.

The answers to these questions are important to children. They are important to theories of delinquency and for policies of delinquency control. This is the setting for the chapters which follow.

University of Miami, Department of Sociology
and
Welfare Planning Council of Dade County,
Director of Research
February, 1963   R.S.S.

ACKNOWLEDGMENTS

This study would not have been possible without the help of many people. Appreciation is expressed to Judge Arthur S. Lane for permission to use the case records of the Mercer County, N. J. Juvenile Court, where Chief Probation Officer Simon J. Falcey, Assistant Chief Rachael F. Owen, and others generously helped in collection of information. Material also was obtained from the Bureau of Juvenile Aid, through former Deputy Police Chief John J. McBride and Captain John A. George.

Enrollment statistics were made available from public and parochial schools by Dr. Richard Robinson, former Superintendent of Schools, Trenton; Mrs. Alice F. Kuser, Director of Educational Extension and Personnel; and Msgr. John J. Endebrock, of the Trenton Diocese. In addition, the U.S. Bureau of the Census provided a special tabulation for this investigation.

Dr. Thorsten Sellin of the Department of Sociology, University of Pennsylvania, gave invaluable help in the formulation and execution of the study. Substantial aid also was given by Drs. Edward P. Hutchinson, Otto Pollak, and Marvin E. Wolfgang of the department. In the initial stages of the project, encouragement and assistance were provided by Mr. Joseph P. Murphy, formerly Chief Probation Officer, Essex County, N.J.; Dr. Ralph Brancale, Director, N.J. State Diagnostic Center; and Mr. Will C. Turnbladh, then Director, National Probation and Parole Association. In addition, editorial advice was given by Dr. Bryce Ryan, University of Miami, and Dr. Erdman B. Palmore, Yale University.

Thanks are also owed to many members of the staffs of

social agencies, libraries, and other organizations. These people gave help in numerous important details.

The most important debt remains to be mentioned—it is to the great assemblage of men and women who developed interest in the problem of juvenile delinquency and the means for studying it. The modest contribution to human welfare contained in this book could not have been made without their work.

TABLE OF CONTENTS

Delinquent Conduct and Broken Homes

CHAPTER ONE

THE IMAGE OF AN ISSUE

X rays first treated cancer in 1896.[1] That same year W. D. Morrison set down judgments on the causes and treatment of juvenile delinquency. From a study of young English delinquents' families, he concluded that, "If a child is of illegitimate parentage . . . if a child is the offspring of callous parents who desert it, if a child has the misfortune to lose one or the other of its parents that child is more likely to become a delinquent than would otherwise be the case."[2] He urged broad reforms to reduce this kind of social distress.

In 1912, Sophonisba Breckinridge and Edith Abbott said, "The misfortunes of being motherless or fatherless make it easy for children in any social stratum to 'get into trouble'," and added that for poor children the misfortune was worst.[3] Three years later, Healy declared, "A very fruitful source of delinquency is found in the separation of parents. . . . The child who is not controlled under the united efforts of both father and mother is at great disadvantage."[4] Later, Healy and Bronner pointed to the one-sided concentration of broken homes among delinquents, in contrast to non-delinquents.[5]

Shideler in 1918 made the first national survey of broken homes and delinquency. The "crippled" family or the broken home, he said, is incapable of functioning properly. It cannot effectively train the child to resist forces opposing the mores, and, he stated, the juvenile there is more likely to become a delinquent than a child in a normal home.[6] In 1924, Mangold declared, "The broken home is probably the most single important proximate cause of delinquency."

A sudden shift in the opinions of most observers came in 1931 with a report by Shaw and McKay.[8] These authors closely compared delinquents and non-delinquents in Cook County, Illinois, and decided that broken homes were not of themselves significant in causing delinquency.[9] This was a turning point. As Weeks and Smith say, "The lack of association found in Chicago between delinquency rates and broken home rates came rather as a shock."[10]

Shortly afterwards came the Social Security Laws of 1935. Through them, disrupted families were physically helped. At the same time, ideas from the field of psychology flowed into those of welfare and social science; the concept of the "inadequate home" began to replace that of the "broken home," though Healy had clearly prepared this ground twenty-five years before.

Teeters and Reinemann have summarized present opinion:[11] "It is not that the home is broken, but rather that the home is inadequate, that really matters. Many mothers, and some fathers, who have lost their mates through separation, divorce, or death, are doing a splendid job of rearing their children. It is not so much the physically broken home as the home that is confused or inadequate . . . that contributes to the high delinquency rates."

Is this the final word? In 1940, Rosenquist wrote,[12] "Not all homes which include both parents are ideal . . . but the probabilities seem to be in favor of the unbroken as against the broken home as a favorable social environment." The Gluecks in 1950 had this to say,[13] "Analysing the nature of all breaks in the family life . . . we find that in every type of family break the delinquent group exceeded the non-delinquent in incidence." In a recent study of delinquents, Penner reports:[14] "The majority of children, almost two out of three, were not living with their natural parents. . . . A

[18]

child whose natural parents have been divorced, separated, committed to a state mental hospital, have deserted or died has experienced a blow that probably affects his psychosocial development."

From the correctional field comes this typical recent statement: "The statistics indicate that children living with but one parent are more likely to become delinquent children by a ratio of two and one-half to one over children living with both parents."[15]

The same views are held on the federal level. In a 1960 document, the Children's Bureau[16] concludes that broken homes are not important in delinquency and refers to the quotation from Teeters and Reinemann stated above. In this Bureau document, we are told that delinquency is high where there are "many unstable families, and a high incidence of illegitimacy and desertion, leading both to maternal employment with inadequate provision for the needs of children and to the lack of a father-figure to provide guidance and affection to the young child."[17] It is also stated, for instance, that ". . . social factors intertwined with delinquency, for example, divorce, desertion and family mobility, are themselves problems of grave concern."[18]

These statements indicate that broken homes continue to be linked in the minds of writers with juvenile misbehavior. Members of the public still hold the broken home to be one of its primary causes. The Governor of the Commonwealth of Pennsylvania, speaking to the education Committee of the U.S. House of Representatives, as reported by the New York *Times*, July 12, 1961, said that the juvenile from the broken home or blighted neighborhood nurtures hostilities stemming from the "emotional torment" of his life; his hostilities become a way of life. "He is society's time bomb, and it is society's responsibility to make certain that the fuse is never lighted."

The discussion of broken homes and delinquency has not burned itself out. Death, desertion, separation, divorce, and other misfortunes to the family circle may shock the observer, but it may be true that the family can subsequently rear children as healthy as those more fortunate—by recouping its unity or through the help of others.

CHAPTER TWO

BEHAVIOR AND FAMILIES

The Workshop of Personality

Every person is shaped by the people with whom he has the closest contact. The intimate contacts occur in primary groups; the less personal, in secondary ones. People in these groupings value certain precepts of behavior, which are the norms and codes that mold the growing person. They determine what he shall be taught, his rewards for learning, and his punishment for deviation.

Of all groups, the family is first. From the outset, parents provide the earliest guidance and discipline for novices in human society. Later, parents supervise the contacts of their children with other members of the community. Outside influences are not under the full control of the family, but adults can evaluate, comment upon, warn about, instruct on, and largely guide the selection of interests. They erect barriers to things of which they disapprove and bring extra pressure to bear against impending deviations. They open ways to things they endorse and give praise for conformity to them.

The rest of the family helps. Siblings may be urged to give the unruly child the cold shoulder, while his elders threaten him and exhort him to be good. A member of a gang tries to break windows after school. He is forbidden to go out at night, and must join a supervised program in a club. A boy is caught stealing money from a parent. He is confronted shamingly by a circle of relatives and is urged to find work and earn his keep. The juvenile learns that group norms are indeed valued. He may test the rules or rebel against them, but he learns them, pleasant or painful as his education may be for all concerned with it.

The family is a group experience in itself. Respect for others' feelings, their prerogatives, role rights, and property rights are the rules of the game. These rules are learned in the family. Here is the boy's first sample of society, the results to be applied in other groups throughout life. Preferred ways of behaving and not behaving are discovered both toward older persons or authority—his parents and toward his peers and juniors—his siblings.

In a healthfully functioning family, the child is nurtured with reasonable security and affection. He develops social attitudes and roles through love, and not restraint alone. Hate and aggression are satisfied or foregone in tolerable ways. Development cannot occur without some frustration, confinement, or bending of the person. Anger at a parent results in a punch at brother or the hurling of a rock, but in a wholesome family, these feelings are absorbed; members are satisfied enough with each other to pass over their troubles. This is meaningful to the child, for his place in the home was not destroyed by such sentiments or acts. The norms he has learned are part of his place and role, and the resilience of the group strengthens his confidence and belief in the patterns he follows and in those assigned to other members. The weakened family is different, for its conflicts actively undermine confidence and add tensions which become problems in themselves.

These are the ways the family, among the child's other groups, teaches the norms of conduct.

Some Definitions and Observations

(Delinquency is the violation of a conduct norm, the violation being prohibited by law.) In moderate cases, these norms, along with others, are enforced by the family, neighbors, peers, and teachers; in the extreme ones, the police, the courts, and correctional institutions must act.

The norms of which we speak vary in compulsion or resistance potentials. This is a concept introduced by Sellin.[1] These variations are expressed by people one to another by the praise or opprobrium they assign to acts. Great deeds are praised more than small kindnesses. Venial sins are damned less than mortal transgressions. These differences allow one to distinguish the "more serious" acts from the "less serious." A youth who violates a norm with high resistance potential has committed a "serious delinquency"; one with low resistance, a "minor delinquency."

The aim of all study of misbehavior is to determine conditions under which any delinquencies occur, or delinquencies with given resistance potentials. We must recognize some of the universal difficulties in their observation.

Only known offenders can be studied. Observation is restricted to juveniles detected, arrested, or sent to court.[2] Among these offenders it must be decided which can be considered to have actually violated the norms. A boy admits to breaking a law but the police and the school, in his particular instance, decide not to send him to court. Was there no violation? "The child," Tappan states, "is not a delinquent unless the court has found him so."[3] It was discovered in this study that authorities often believe, especially of early delinquents, that warnings and reprimands are a sufficient deterrent. Likewise, with admitted guilt, the judge may dismiss a case, feeling that court appearance alone was punishment enough.

For these reasons, charged offenses, and not solely those adjudicated, were used in the present investigation. The few instances in which the court or court personnel found the police charges to be clearly incorrect were eliminated.[4]

It may be objected that not all social classes agree with

the prohibitions of the delinquency norms, which are in large part the precepts of the law-enforcing classes. However, Kvaraceus and Miller say the "street corner kids" know the legal sanctions very well, motivated as they may be in other directions.[5] This subject has been well reviewed by Barron;[6] many studies, such as those by Hartshorne and May, show that children of all shades of behavior know what is supposed to be right and that they know if they get caught they may be punished more severely for violating strict norms than for weak ones.

The Study of Delinquency Causation

The study of delinquency determines conditions under which misbehavior occurs. By the word "occurrence" may be meant two things. It may mean the presence or absence of a condition, to be observed on an all-or-none basis as a status and reported in terms of incidence or rates. "Occurrence" may also refer to the strength of the manifestation of a phenomenon, which is reported in terms of its average intensity, or the proportion of strong instances as against the weak.

Most studies of broken homes have used the term "delinquent" on the all-or-none status basis. The object has been to relate the presence or absence of the status to the presence or absence of broken homes. There is the other approach. (If broken homes are no less effective in social control than are unbroken ones, there should be the same proportion of serious offenses among offenders from each. This is the method used in this book.)

These two approaches are not unrelated. The group with stronger controls will have the lower delinquency rate. This connection has been described by Reckless and by Reiss.[7] Earlier Sterne had shown that parolees for whom guidance and aid were stressed, for instance, by the prison psychologist, violated parole in smaller proportion than those without such a recommendation. "Since the parole officer was given the prognosis together with a brief history and results of the man's tests, he was careful, it may be assumed, in the supervision of those men considered poor risks or needing special guidance."[8] As to the relation of family discipline itself to incidence, the Gluecks' study may be cited.[9] Poor control was more common in the families of the delinquents than in those of the non-delinquents.

What is the relation of delinquency rate to seriousness? Let us consider the juvenile's situation. Accepted group goals are not the only ones a boy knows, especially in city areas with high delinquency rates where gang mates, interesting girl friends, and successful adult criminals offer examples of other rewards. Which shall a boy pursue?

In a well-functioning group, these deviant goals are put aside out of loyalty to one's associates, or are suppressed by their opposition. If a boy pushes to satisfy such desires, severe restraint, and, conflict within himself may ensue. With these come antagonism to control, loss of pleasure in conformity, and finally, in some cases, a reversal of values. Good becomes bad, and bad becomes good. This is typical of the delinquent gang. A youth need not be a member of such a band; he can experience these feelings on his own;[10] but whether alone or in company, the pattern which has developed is highly charged with emotion.

Where controls are lax, deviation has little meaning; here it means everything to the would-be offender. When he becomes an actual offender, his exaggerated feelings cause him to act in an exaggerated way, to "go overboard." At the same time, what he finally does may become a means of self-assertion by which he seeks to punish his restrainers. He chooses the most serious act of which he is capable. In addition, his forbidden wishes have aggravated his guilt feelings, which demand punishment; the worse the act, the greater the punishment to the group and, in return, to him. Therefore, the more effective the control of delinquency, the worse the eventuating delinquencies.

This boy echoes the folklore "renegade son of the minister." He is illustrated in many studies. Walters[11] shows that among drinkers alcoholism is associated more highly with an abstinence than a non-abstinence background. Agreement between parents on religion and the degree of their activity in church, especially that of the mother, is also associated with alcoholism in their offspring. Bacon[12] compares the consequences of drinking in two groups. Among Orthodox Jews the consumption of liquor involves little feeling, while among Mormons, it is taboo and its use is most highly charged with significance. Among Jewish drinkers, there is little alcoholism. The proportion is much greater among Mormon drinkers, to whom breaking the norm is so meaningful.

Christensen compares the aftereffects of premarital pregnancies among couples taken from different backgrounds.[13] In Denmark, forced marriages are not considered dishonorable; the couples wed and their later divorce rate is low. Among comparable American pairs, the ensuing divorce rate is higher. These partings are probably the result of face-saving legitimizations, but they indicate that once the norms have been ruptured, the violation is likely to be compounded by making it obvious that the marriage was forced. Similarly, Elliott found that female sex offenders from "good" homes made poorer later adjustment than did other girls.[14]

It is also appropriate to mention the remarks that Cohen makes about the middle-class boy who revolts against the domination masked in his "good" mother's affection. He breaks this bond by doing something bad, to assert his masculinity.[15]

In the present study, other evidence appeared which showed that strict control is associated with more serious acts. Two groups committed serious offenses in proportions significantly above the average. These were devout Protestant boys and boys whose parents were born abroad. This second set of youngsters presumably was more strictly disciplined at home. Three groups with lax control committed, by contrast, a significantly lower than average proportion of serious acts. These were non-devout Protestant boys, boys whose parents had different religious affiliations, and boys with poor home supervision.[16] Details are given in later pages.

In conclusion, this study analyzes the relation of the strength of social control to the seriousness of the deviant act. Other studies have analyzed its relation to delinquency incidence. These two approaches merely examine the same problem in different ways.

Broken Homes and Delinquency

A broken home in our culture is defined as a household in which the child has been deprived of one or both natural parents by death, divorce, separation, or other cause, or in which the illegitimate father was never present. It remains to be shown that a break in the home could impair the effectiveness of rearing children and thus alter the force of social control. Reasons will first be given for expecting such impairment, and then, for not expecting it.

When a parent is absent, supervision may be reduced. Guidance, advice, and control may lessen and barriers to delinquent friendships may weaken. The backing of family authority may decline; by default the boy can drift into delinquent conduct.

Training may dwindle sharply. The boy is corrected less often for testing the norms and he is tutored less forcefully in the mores. One important model for action, the mother or father, is gone. Loyalty to the family may be impaired, for there is a gap in the circle, and this gap perhaps is the mark of preceding conflict; but whatever has brought the loss, the effectiveness of guidance has been diminished.

If a broken home makes it harder to rear a child, the difficulty should not be the same for all kinds of breaks. Taft says, "Death is a fairly normal experience. It may indeed remove a kind father's influence and often means economic hardship. But it involves no connotation of friction such as is involved in separation, divorce and desertion."[17]

Families broken by divorce, separation, and desertion have undergone a period of contention and conflict. Such boys have seen the action resulting from animosity and have heard ill words spoken of their fathers or mothers. If the father walked out when the boy was small, the mother has communicated her grudge to the son. These animadversions undermine belief in the binding force of conventions; and the fact that a parent broke the family union, whose preservation is held as a sacred value, may weaken respect for social sanctions.

This reasoning would lead to a prediction that boys from broken homes would commit a larger proportion of less serious offenses than boys from average homes, and that those from homes broken by conflict—that is, divorce, separation, and desertion—would commit the largest proportion of such acts.

There are, conversely, grounds to believe that broken homes are no worse than average. The family and home as an association may be fractured, though physically intact. Parents in an unbroken home may fail in their duties or perform them miserably; while in a broken home, the remaining parent may take over and improve on the departed's role.[18] Step-parents may fill the place. The surrogate may be less interested than the real parent in the child, and the boy may say, "Don't tell me—you're not my real father," but this is not always so. And further, uncles, aunts, grandparents, and friends may assume important roles as substitute parents which they would not otherwise have performed. Divorce or desertion may end conflict and restore peace. Either may be a constructive step in the life of a youth and in his respect for the mores.

In summary, there are reasons to believe that a break in the family makes it harder to guide and control the child. There are also reasons to believe that full or partial compensation for the break may be made.

It is the task of this book to see whether a break is in fact a detriment to the child. Past studies will first be reviewed, and then the results of this study will be presented.

CHAPTER THREE

SOME EARLIER STUDIES

The relation of broken homes to delinquency has been discussed for at least the past seventy years. The majority of studies has been on delinquency incidence; there is, in fact, almost nothing on the seriousness of the delinquency, although material on it may be abstracted from certain reports. No investigation has combined the approaches by inquiring, for instance, about rates of serious offenses by type of home situation.

Earlier works are reviewed here. These do not represent all that have appeared. Reviews of those on incidence include eight which employed control groups, or appropriate portions of them; three studies providing material on seriousness are reported.

Studies of Incidence

Shideler presented a pioneer survey in 1918, of 7,557 white and Negro boys and 41 girls in industrial schools and reformatories throughout the United States.[1]

He said: "The purpose of this paper is to present in a summary way a comparative study of family disintegration as related to juvenile delinquency. Several such studies have been made in certain cities or institutions, but very few if any, have investigated the factor of parental and conjugal conditions in any comprehensive fashion. The present study is an attempt, as far as possible, to gather statistical facts, representing the United States as a whole, bearing on the relation of family disintegration to juvenile delinquency."[2]

Cases were classed by type of home. Comparison estimates were made of the national rates of juvenile family situations, based on the census. A proportion of 51.8 per cent broken homes among the delinquents was found. This was much greater than the estimated 25.3 per cent in the general juvenile population. The greatest disparity was found in the proportions of break by separation.

The first major attempt at a controlled comparison was made by Slawson and published in 1926. Sixteen hundred and forty-nine boys in New York State institutions were contrasted to 3,198 school children in New York City.[3] No variables were held constant, but the two groups were considered alike. Slawson said that boys in Public School Number 11, totaling 738, resembled the delinquents the most.[4] Comparisons here are restricted solely to boys from that school.

Among the delinquents, 54.8 per cent had unbroken homes; among non-delinquents, 69.7 per cent.[5] The difference is 14.9 per cent ± 2.2 per cent. Were any of the different types of breaks more prevalent among the delinquents than the non-delinquents? Each pair of breaks was compared.[6]

In Table 1, "n" means that the percentages differed insignificantly between delinquents and non-delinquents. "S" means that they differed significantly at the five per cent level or less. There were significantly more delinquents with two parents dead than with only the father dead. Comment on these results, and others, will be reserved until all the studies have been reviewed.

(Elliott and Merrill[7] state in their book *Social Disorganization* that: "The family background of the child, more than any other factor, tends to militate against his growing up successfully without conflict with the law.)In fact, the major handicap of the delinquent child is that he has not chosen

TABLE 1

SLAWSON'S CASES COMPARED FOR SIGNIFICANCES OF
FAMILY DIFFERENCES

	Both Dead	Mother Dead	Separated, Divorced	Father Dead
Delinquents	3.3%	14.4%	9.7%	17.8%
Non-delinquents	1.3%	8.0%	6.2%	14.8%
Both dead		n	n	S
Mother dead			n	S
Separated, divorced				n

his family wisely!" In test of the relation of broken homes to this factor, they compare a group of delinquents studied by Elliott[8] and of non-delinquents studied by Ormsbee.[9]

The delinquents consisted of 203 white girls at Sleighton Farms, Pennsylvania, committed between 1913 and 1915. All were sex offenders except five charged with larceny alone and two who were dependent. The non-delinquents were 263 white girls attending Philadelphia continuation schools, while working, during 1923 and 1924.

Text and tables show that girls were well matched for color, age, residence, birthplace of parents, girls' own nativity, school retardation, and type of employment. The fathers of the delinquents were mostly unskilled laborers; those of the control group were not described. There was a difference in time of observation, noted above.

Among the delinquents, 47.8 per cent had unbroken homes; in the comparison group, 77.6 per cent. The difference is 29.8 per cent ± 4.4 per cent. Differences between breaks were analyzed in the same manner as in the review of Slawson's study. There was one significant discrepancy: death of mother was significantly higher among the delinquents than death of father.

In 1931 the study by Shaw and McKay appeared. They said, "In the studies of the problem of juvenile delinquency, the family has received more attention than any other social institution. Particular emphasis has been placed upon family disorganization or the 'broken home.' . . . The findings of this study . . . establish certain norms that would be valuable, in Chicago at least, in interpreting the significance of the incidence of broken homes found in any series of juvenile delinquents. . . . We are interested . . . in broken homes regardless of the cause of the break. . . . It is entirely possible that the break in the home may be advantageous or desirable from the point of view of the boy, but that is not our concern in this chapter."[10]

Delinquents were 1,675 boys, Negro and white, aged ten to seventeen who appeared in Cook County Court in 1929. They were mainly the serious offenders, since the police probation officer system had skimmed off most of the others. Non-delinquents were 7,278 schoolboys, who came from twenty-nine public schools which were chosen to reflect different areas and ethnic groups, and who were personally interviewed.

Ethnic classifications were important in this study. Delinquents were classified by their fathers; schoolboys, by both parents; there was a "mixed" group among them. Delinquency rates were also important. Rates were based on the home addresses of 8,141 first court appearances, 1917-23, in the square mile about each school; these were expressed as rates of boys ten to fifteen in these squares.

The total broken home rate for schoolboys was 29.0 per cent. The correlation between broken homes in individual schools and their area delinquency rates was 0.19 per cent ± 0.12 per cent, which appeared to show a complete lack of relation. This is not certain: area broken home rates were based on the family conditions of the boys attending schools in them, while delinquency rates were based on the arrests of boys living in these areas. This may be sound for the lower grades, but older boys may travel some distance from home to class. Also, parochial schools were excluded, and the arrests counted had occurred some six to twelve years earlier. Finally, the correlations were not personal, but ecological; and as Robinson and others have shown, such indices may create false connections or obscure real ones.[11]

Shaw and McKay found that broken homes were much more prevalent in some groups of schoolboys than in others. For Negroes, the rate was 46.0 per cent; for Jews, 16.3 per cent. The percentages also varied by age. Linear age regressions were plotted, producing an adjusted Negro rate of 48.7 per cent, and a Jewish rate of 19.8 per cent, for example. For the total, the new figure was 30.9 per cent. These adjustments were made only for the schoolboys, not for the delinquents.

The ethnic composition of the delinquent and control groups differed. The over-all rate for the latter was corrected; each cell in the non-delinquent group was weighted according to the proportion of boys by age and ethnic group in the delinquent group, and the result was to increase the non-delinquent rate from 30.9 per cent to 36.1 per cent. The delinquent rate, 42.5 per cent, was 1.18 times larger.

Shaw and McKay presented these results in bold typography and believed them to show that broken homes as such were not an important factor in delinquency causation.[12] This finding has been discussed by many persons. Maller noted that there was in fact a difference of 6.4 per cent, which is 5.7 times its probable error.[13] Toby observed that if the delinquents had been standardized to the schoolboy age and ethnic composition, instead of the other way around as done by Shaw and McKay, the figures would have been 40 per cent for delinquents and 29 per cent for the controls, or 1 to 1.38.[14] It was noted by Colcord[15] and by Shulman[16] that type of break was not considered. Maller says that there may have been some delinquents in the control group,[17] but Shaw and McKay say that this error was small.[18]

Shaw and McKay also compared the rates of broken homes among the delinquents to the delinquency rates of the areas in which they lived.[19] For the areas with low, intermediate, and high delinquency rates, the proportions of broken homes among the boys were 41.9 per cent, 42.5 per cent and 43.2 per cent. The meaning of this finding is not clear. It was pointed out in an earlier paragraph that there was a time lag of six to twelve years between the offenses on which the rates were based and the study of the broken homes. The findings do show, in any case, that the incidence of broken homes among delinquents was the same in all types of areas.

A study of Hodgkiss published in 1933 carried the methods used by Shaw and McKay to higher refinement.[20] Delinquent subjects included 363 of the 1,400 female petitions to the Cook County Juvenile Court in 1928, 1929, 1930, and part of 1931. The largest ethnic groups, those with Polish, Negro, and native white fathers, were taken; girls over sixteen were excluded, for better matching to controls.

The non-delinquents came from 835 girls in nine public and continuation schools to whom family status questionnaires were given; those known as delinquents by teachers or principals were eliminated. A random sample equal in size to the delinquent group was taken from each age among the selected ethnic groups. Each of the final delinquent and control groups was close to the over-all average of 14.7 years of age.

A strong difference in broken homes was found. The delinquents had 66.9 per cent; the non-delinquents, 44.8 per cent. This difference is 22.1 per cent ± 3.6 per cent. Four breaks—parents apart and mother, father, or both dead—were specified. Tests explained in Appendix B in this book showed no significant disparities among them.

Hodgkiss believed that the association found in her cases between broken homes and delinquency might have reflected the work of social agencies, for Shaw had noted that those organizations worked actively with disrupted families and perhaps channeled the delinquent daughters to court.

Weeks and Smith sought to see if what Shaw and McKay had found in Chicago applied in Spokane as well. They wrote, "It is recognized that broken homes alone do not cause delinquency, as behavior is a product of the total situation. But how close an association is there between delinquency and broken homes when certain other factors are held constant? . . . It seems surprising that Shaw and McKay should find such a low correlation. . . . Do the findings in Spokane support these conclusions?"[21]

The delinquents were 326 male juveniles appearing in court in Spokane in 1937, while controls were 2,119 boys, fourteen to eighteen, in five Spokane secondary public schools, data on whom were got by questionnaires. All reporting that they had been arrested were dropped. Broken homes among the schoolboys had no ethnic trends. The standardizations made by Shaw and McKay were not performed.

Ecological correlations were prepared, based on the relations between the delinquency rates in each of the thirty-six school districts and the characteristics of the boys in the schools or their families. Reservations about such techniques expressed in the discussion of the Shaw and McKay report also apply here; however, these were the results: delinquency and broken homes, .38 ± .15; homes rented and delinquency, .49 ± .13; rentals and delinquency, broken homes partialed out, .38 ± .15; delinquency and foreign-born, .02 ± .18; delinquency and heads of family unemployed, .14 ± .17. Three districts deviated sharply from the others in the relation of broken homes and delinquency. One had many arrests for "childish pranks"; another had a large Jewish population with little delinquency, and a third had a heterogeneous population. These three removed, the relation between broken homes and delinquency became .61 ± .12.

Homes broken voluntarily and involuntarily were separated from each other. For those with voluntary breaks, the correlation with delinquency was .40 ± .15, which hardly differed from that for the total, or .38 ± .15. The classification of breaks may have been too broad; for example, in other studies, there was a much closer relation between delinquency and death of mother than between it and death of father. Weeks and Smith combined these.

When rental of homes was partialed out, the ecological correlation between delinquency and broken homes dropped to .06 ± .18. A table brings out that this was the product of an association between rentals and delinquency. Rental of homes among the families of the delinquents was more frequent than among those of the controls by 17.8 per cent (± 3.8 per cent). However, among the non-rental families, there was a significantly higher proportion of broken homes than among the delinquents. Among the renters, there was no significant difference. There is a complex relation in this material, which was not explained.

The fathers' occupations were analyzed. In both the white-collar and laborer-unemployed groups, there were equal percentages of broken homes among delinquents. But most boys from broken homes are not with their fathers; one should consider not the father's job, but that of the head of the home, whoever that is.

In the decade following this study, two other important investigations appeared. These were *The Young Delinquent,* by Cyril Burt[22] and *Juvenile Delinquency and the School,* by William C. Kvaraceus.[23] Burt provides material relevant to the problems discussed here, but categories in his tabulations appear to overlap. Kvaraceus does not provide a control group, and is therefore not included in this review.

In 1950, a major study by the Gluecks appeared. The

Gluecks here declared, as a result of what they found, that "the delinquent boys, far more than the non-delinquents, grew up in a family atmosphere not conducive to the development of emotionally well-integrated, happy youngsters, conditioned to obedience to legitimate authority."[24]

Five hundred delinquents and five hundred non-delinquents were compared. The offenders were 493 male admissions to two Massachusetts correctional schools and seven non-institutional cases. The boys studied came from pre-selected deteriorated or underprivileged high-delinquency areas in Boston, and were judged to be serious and persistent offenders; a few boys were from outside areas.

Five hundred non-delinquents, from whom delinquents had been screened (a few with single minor infractions were retained) were matched with the delinquents. The matching was good for average age and intelligence. Ethnic pairing was based on the ultimate origins of parents or grandparents. Leeway was allowed: Polish was matched to Lithuanian and French to French Canadian, and so on. Boys were not paired by neighborhood. The final groups were not well equated for type of area. The non-delinquents lived in better sections.[25] These differences were claimed to have "no significance";[26] yet there were 18.6 per cent more delinquents than controls in interstitial areas; this is 6.1 times its standard error. Delinquents had moved more frequently,[27] had families receiving more social service,[28] which were less well off economically[29] and which had heads with lower grade occupations.[30] On the other hand, types of dwellings and average rentals did not differ significantly.[31] Ratings of the two blocks square about each home as to vice centers and opportunities for wholesome recreation were close.[32] Delinquency rates in the areas of their homes were not materially different.[33] The factor of gang membership was ignored. Reiss has criticized this omission.[34] It is also to be noted that delinquents and controls were compared on many factors, but none was held constant in broken home comparisons. For this reason, detailed attention has been given to the matching of groups.

Delinquents and controls were compared according to the nature of the first breaks in their homes.[35] In all, 60.4 per cent of the delinquent homes were broken; of the non-delinquent, 34.2 per cent. This is a difference of 26.2 per cent ± 3.0 per cent. Five specific categories of broken homes were utilized: mother or father dead; one or both deserted boy; permanently separated or divorced; never married and soon abandoned boy; other abnormal situation. Differences among these were analyzed by the method of Appendix B. Results are shown in Table 2. Among the significant figures, illegitimacy and desertion were most closely associated with delinquency; parents separated or divorced, the least closely.

TABLE 2

THE GLUECKS' CASES COMPARED FOR SIGNIFICANCES OF FAMILY DIFFERENCES

	Unmarried	Deserted	Other	Dead	Separated, Divorced
Delinquents	4.8%	14.8%	20.8%	12.4%	7.6%
Non-delinquents	1.0%	5.4%	10.0%	10.6%	7.2%
Unmarried		n	n	S	S
Deserted			n	S	S
Other				S	S
Dead					n

The results are difficult to interpret. Death of mother and father were combined. These showed differences in other studies when separately examined. Other comments appear later in this chapter.

The final study of incidence to be considered was published by Monahan in 1957. He states, "For the social analyst, the broken home may be regarded either as a symptom or as a consequence of a larger process, but for the child it becomes a social fact with which he has to abide. . . . That so many children surpass this handicap is an exemplification of their own resilience and a demonstration of the presence of other forces acting towards the child's socialization in the community, rather than a proof of the unimportance of normal family life. . . ."[36]

His comparisons were not between delinquents and non-delinquents, but between those appearing once and more than once in court. Subjects included 36,245 boys and girls, white and non-white, representing 44,448 appearances in the Philadelphia Municipal Court, 1949-54. Information was obtained from case records, which in some instances were based on the juveniles' personal statements about their families. Double counting of individuals was eliminated within single years of the five-year span.

Distinction of family types was superior to that of all other studies (see Table 3 for their listing). The types of breaks occurred in different proportions and ranks in the sex and color groups. However, there was a greater proportion of repeat appearances in every type of broken home than in unbroken homes in every group and in all instances save one. This was among Negro boys of divorce, but the difference there was not statistically significant.

For white boys, detailed comparisons are made here. There were in this group 11,244 first appearances and 4,323 repeaters. Of the repeaters, 41.3 per cent had broken homes; of the single appearances, 26.9 per cent. This difference is significant at the one per cent level. Comparisons were made among types of breaks, as outlined in Appendix B. Table 3 shows that repeated appearances were significantly fewer among those with both parents dead than among those with

TABLE 3

MONAHAN'S CASES COMPARED FOR SIGNIFICANCES OF FAMILY DIFFERENCES

	Mother Deserted	Un-married	Father Deserted	Apart	Mother Dead	Parents Divorced	Father Dead	Both Dead	Both Deserted
First appearances	0.2%	1.6%	0.7%	7.9%	2.9%	5.3%	7.7%	0.5%	0.1%
Repeaters	0.5%	3.6%	1.4%	12.9%	4.6%	8.1%	9.5%	0.6%	0.1%
Mother Deserted		n	n	n	n	n	n	n*	n
Parents Unmarried			n	S	S	S	S	S	n
Father Deserted				n	S	n	S	n	n
Parents Apart					n	n	S	n	n
Mother Dead						n	S	n	n
Parents Divorced							S	n	n
Father Dead								n	n
Both Parents Dead									n

* P: .057

unmarried parents. In Monahan's report, father dead varied insignificantly from both parents dead. These were at antipodes in other investigations.

Monahan also examined the relation between the presence of step-parents and repeated appearances. For some groups, such as white male orphans, there was a positive connection; while for white boys with divorced mothers, it was negative. In any case, here is a factor which warrants attention.

Studies of Seriousness

Past material on this subject is hard to find. Some authors, however, have specified the acts the children committed, and thus it is possible to relate offense to family situation. In reporting their work here, the categories of "serious" and "minor" acts are used in the manner described in Chapter V.

Breckinridge and Abbott presented, in a study published in 1912, portraits of the delinquency careers of one hundred boys.[37] These sketches are given as typical of the 584 for whom family schedules were obtained in the authors' famous report on Cook County Court cases. From the portraits it is possible to derive the family conditions at first-mentioned appearance in court. It was found that of forty-eight boys with unbroken homes, twenty-eight appeared for serious acts. Of fifty-two from broken homes, thirty appeared for such offenses. There is practically no difference; no attempt was made to classify cases by type of break.

A Russell Sage Foundation report of 1914 provides a tabulation of the family situations of children appearing in the New York Court for the year 1913.[38] The report divided cases into two groups: juvenile delinquents and special proceedings. The second included truants, incorrigibles, disorderly juveniles, and neglected children. This is a grouping roughly similar to that used in the present study under the heading "minor offenses," except for neglected children who are not included at all. Among the Russell Sage cases, boys totaled 2,542. Of these, 1,669 were from unbroken homes, and 61.3 per cent of this number were "juvenile delinquents." There were 873 from broken homes, with 69.8 per cent "delinquents." Among girls there were 133 from unbroken homes and 111 from broken ones. "Delinquents" among these were 21.8 per cent and 10.8 per cent respectively. The inclusion of neglected children may account for these inconsistent differences. No conclusions can be drawn from the figures. The Russell Sage report details offenders by family situations; however, the data do not warrant analysis.

In comparing the homes of boys and girls to their types of offenses, Weeks has provided data which allow a comparison of the seriousness of the boys' acts.[39] Cases consisted of juveniles appearing, about 1940, before the Spokane Juvenile Court. Family situations were divided among those unbroken, broken voluntarily, and broken involuntarily. The unbroken family boys numbered 238; the voluntary break group, 92, the involuntary, 61. The respective percentages of serious offenses were 44.5, 39.2, and 44.5. The differences are insignificant.

What Do the Data Mean?

What is learned from the studies reviewed?

Are there more minor offenses among juveniles from broken homes? Three reports were cited on this; the results were inconclusive.

Is there a greater incidence of delinquency among juveniles from broken homes? There appears to be a strong relation among the cases investigated, but before accepting this conclusion, let other evidence be considered.

Slawson provided information which showed that boys from broken homes were sent to institutions more readily than those whose homes were whole. The average number of arrests before commitment varied widely according to family situation. Among House of Refuge cases the mean for boys with parents together was 3.63; for those with parents separated or divorced, 3.21; mother or father dead, 3.19; both dead, 2.89.[40]

Slawson also computed the "severity of delinquent career" prior to commitment,[41] using scores derived from the number of days of imprisonment or dollar fines adults might have received for given offenses. At the House of Refuge, boys with parents together had an "average severity" score of 23.24; separated or divorced, 20.58; father or mother dead, 19.95; both dead, 15.68. The more disadvantaged boys were committed more easily, perhaps with intent to help them; but is Slawson's association of broken homes with delinquency or with institutionalization?

This raises a serious question about the transition from the known association with institutionalization to the assumed association with delinquency. The same question must color the interpretation of studies by the Gluecks, by Elliott and Ormsbee, and by Shideler, and the studies of court appearances by Hodgkiss, Monahan, Weeks and Smith, and Shaw and McKay. Hodgkiss found an association between broken homes and delinquency among girls referred to court. Shaw suggested that this reflected the work of social agencies. This was not proved, yet not refuted. Monahan found a connection between the court's own handling of cases and broken homes; a similar bias may have existed in the anterior actions of the police who must first have made the decisions to send the juveniles to court. Taking white boys (representative of all groups), there were 27.9 per cent broken homes among first appearances. Some of these were adjusted by the staff; some were held for court. In the first group there were 21.6 per cent broken homes; in the second, 35.0 per cent.[42] It is evident that administrative procedure was influenced by the family situation.

What of types of breaks? It may be superfluous to comment on them, but it is to be noted that the studies, so far as they are comparable, disagreed widely on the degree of association of different breaks with delinquency (or institutionalization or court appearance). In four studies, significant differences were found among the types of ruptures. Slawson found the highest significant association among juveniles with both parents dead, lowest among those with father dead. For Elliott and Ormsbee the highest was mother dead; lowest, father dead. For the Gluecks it was unmarried, and separated or divorced; and for Monahan, unmarried and both dead. Hodgkiss, and Weeks and Smith revealed no significant differences. Tests could not be made of Shideler's material, and Shaw and McKay did not differentiate types of breaks. These varied findings indicate that types of breaks may be important, but they offer no clear guide to their rank order.

Some Methodological Remarks

It is useful to examine prior reports to determine the best means of conducting a new study.

In any study of broken homes, the object is to see if they are a causative or antecedent condition. In ecological analyses, two rates are compared for each area: broken homes and delinquency. It is shown by Robinson and others,[43] as mentioned before, that ecological correlations may be high but do not prove that delinquents are the ones who came from broken homes. Therefore, studies such as those by Shaw and McKay and by Weeks and Smith may be inconclusive.

In studies of individuals, it may be found that delinquents have a larger proportion of broken homes than do non-delinquents. Is it known that their homes were broken before they became deviants? If not, how may any weight be assigned to the break? Past studies have ignored this point.

In this study twelve out of 368 boys from unbroken homes underwent a break between first offense and first court referral. This covered the boys considered only at first appearance; if they had been observed in later careers, as in most other investigations, the precedence of a break would be an even more important factor.

The failure of past studies to differentiate carefully, if at all, between types of broken homes, has been pointed out. The time when the break occurred and with whom the juvenile then went to live have been largely neglected. Also, one rupture may follow another, as divorce upon desertion, or death of step-mother upon divorce. Each of these aspects is considered in this investigation.

Controls have not been fully applied in earlier investigations; other variables have been considered in relation to delinquency, but not in broken home analyses. In some studies, limited controls have been used. The research reported in the following chapters has employed all controls for which reliable data could be obtained.

To Sum Up

The results of previous reports are ambiguous because of unresolved uncertainties in sources of data and some shortcomings in the methods of analysis used.

CHAPTER FOUR

DEFINING THE UNIVERSE

The broad purpose of the research reported on the pages *purpose* which follow is to see whether or not broken homes affect delinquent behavior. How does the investigator determine this influence? It must be sought in a suitable universe of cases in which the relation of family situations to conduct can be observed.

The Locus of Observation

The variables of situation and action must have freedom to operate. This freedom is greatest at the time of first offense. After the initial infraction, additional factors enter the scene. The boy is now a "delinquent." This changes his own ideas of himself, his family, his peers, his school, and his neighborhood, described by Wattenburg.[1] The family tries harder to labor with the boy. The success or failure of the court as an authority and the boy's experience with the police and with institutions intervene between him and his family. His new skills in law-breaking affect his conception of himself. To eliminate these great complexities, first offenses were chosen for observation. The dynamics of later influences is an important area of study, as are the motives for the second, third, and following offenses. Yet analysis of the first offense will help guide inquiry into other instances.

[49]

Sources of Cases

In thinking of a study of delinquents, these four sources of information on the history or present situation of individuals might be envisioned: (1) records of institutionalized cases; (2) records of all cases appearing before the court; (3) records of all juveniles arrested; (4) records of all delinquents arrested or not.

The ideal study would be that of all delinquents, arrested or not, which is impossible. Nor is it possible to substitute delinquencies known to the police, for the age of the offender is not shown by the act, nor for that matter are the actor's sex, color, social status, or personal history—all factors which are essential to the evaluation of motivation.

Institutional records provide a wealth of data on each case; in fact, a pilot analysis for this study was made at the New Jersey State Diagnostic Center. However, it is well known that institutionalized cases are highly selected, and this cannot be ignored in the final results.[2]

Juveniles arrested bring one closer to the totality of delinquents than do other available sources. In the city where the study was made, Trenton, New Jersey, the Bureau of Juvenile Aid of the police department handles all young offenders. However, this source was not used, because certain important factors, including family composition, the past history of the home, intelligence, household mobility, quality of supervision, parent's religion, and other data are not recorded by the police.

The source used was the file of juveniles appearing before the court. Cases reaching court are generally the more troublesome ones and form a valid sample, since the study of a social problem such as delinquency can well attend to its more serious manifestations. In 1957, a typical year in Trenton, 58.9 per cent of juvenile arrests were for serious offenses.[3] Of all appearances before the court in 1957, 72.3

per cent were serious cases.[4] 71.3 per cent of this study's cases were of this kind at first appearance in court.

Juvenile court data in several cities were considered, but Trenton, New Jersey, was selected. All juveniles before the Juvenile Court of that city are investigated by the Probation Department, which keeps good records. They are compiled from thorough field visits, police records, Social Service Exchange clearances, social agency information, school reports, and—where necessary—psychiatric evaluations and other data. For some cases, these records were supplemented by information from the Exchange, the Trenton Department of Welfare, the Bureau of Juvenile Aid, the Trenton Board of Education, the New Jersey Department of Institutions and Agencies, and other social agencies. From these sources were obtained, for example, the date of the mother's death or the location of a previous residence; a few cases with major omissions were not used.

A data sheet was devised, based on extensive preliminary testing. Items were selected which were meaningful and on which information could be obtained in almost all cases and which could be expressed in objective terms.

Selection for Uniformity

In New Jersey, juvenile courts cover all persons under eighteen brought before the court on petition. Murder and like acts may be referred to adult courts; no such case was found. Among the totality of juvenile court cases, selection was made. Only white boys were included, for they formed the largest single group of delinquents. There is some evidence that broken homes and delinquency are more closely associated among girls, but female cases were too few to permit control of the additional variables that their inclusion would have required. Similarly, Negro cases were excluded. Sex and race are discussed in more detail in a later chapter.

Six specific family situations were included: unbroken, father dead, mother dead, parents divorced, parents separated, and father deserted; others were too few in number to analyze. Each broken home was classified according to the first break in that family. The record of each unbroken home was examined to ensure that the family was intact at the first offense of the boy, and of these cases, every fourth one, or a total of 25 per cent, was recorded for analysis.

The Trenton court covers all of Mercer County. Some boys appearing in it may have committed their first offense in municipalities adjacent to Trenton, or, if recidivists, in other counties. Only juveniles residing in Trenton at their first offense were included in this study. This was done because rates of arrests in areas of residence were used as a control, and these could be computed for Trenton, while information requisite for them was not available from other places. Also, restriction to Trenton minimized differentials between the city and outlying areas in the handling of offenders by the police and schools.

Limiting cases to Trenton reduced the available number. To enlarge the group, the selection period was extended backwards. Broken homes have been considered a problem in all years, and there has been no period in which a claim for their effect was not made. Consequently, first arrests, October 7, 1937, through June 30, 1959, were used. The Bureau of Juvenile Aid, and new policies governing it, were established by law effective the earlier date, and as to the latter, case collection terminated in August, 1959.

Traffic violators were excluded, for New Jersey law says that any traffic offender seventeen years of age and over with a valid driver's license charged with speeding, passing a light, illegal parking, etc., shall be heard in Police Court. Records of seventeen-year-old traffic violators would not appear in the juvenile court files, unless they were persistent offenders and were sent in as incorrigibles. Such cases would

be rare. Police Court records contain only personal identifi-
cation, offense, and previous record, and therefore could
not be used to supplement the under-seventeen traffic offenders who did appear in the juvenile court and its files.
Because of the legal exclusion of those over sixteen—and
these formed the largest juvenile traffic group—none of them
was included.

The juvenile court age changed during the period covered
by the study, and some court practices underwent alteration
in the same period. These are discussed as controlled variables in a later chapter.

Finally, a few other unusual cases were excluded, as explained below.

In total, 1,347 cases of white boys appearing before the
court during the period covered by the study and resident
in Trenton at the time of their first offense were considered
for inclusion. Ten hundred and fifty were included and
297 were excluded:

Included

Broken homes (father dead, mother dead, parents di- vorced, parents separated, father deserted)	326
Unbroken homes (25 per cent, or 181, actually recorded for analysis)	724
Total	1,050

Excluded

Traffic violation was first or only offense	29
Case incomplete or could not be found (includes those known to exist from court files or references, but not located during the study)	91
Case not delinquent (charge proven to be incorrect; no other charge or offense known)	38
Special status (illegitimate, 45; adopted, 10)	55
Other situations (father drafted, 4; father institutional- ized, 14; mother institutionalized, 13; mother deserted, 22; both parents deserted, 6; both parents dead, 4; other unusual situation, 21)	84
Total	297

There were forty-five illegitimate boys, but they did not form a homogeneous group and were not used. Some were foundlings; some, the products of premarital pregnancies of now stable families; some, the results of adultery. The twenty-one "other unusual situations" included, for example, a home in which the father ate with the family, but lived in his own home elsewhere; a boy whose father had married while escaped from prison and who was taken back; a boy whose mother died, whose step-father and step-mother were jailed, and who was living with a brother.

Very few boys were found who became delinquents while their fathers were in the armed services. This was considered surprising. Some had fathers in uniform when the boys were small. Little information was available on these events. However, Hill[5] found no great evidence of child maladjustment caused by the draft of the male parent. He found that most children recuperated well from the deprivation of the father's presence, upon his return, except in families disorganized before he went away.

Conclusion

This study covered white boys who resided in Trenton, New Jersey, a typical urban area, at their first offenses and who then or later appeared in the Mercer County Juvenile Court.[6] They constitute a group who committed acts more serious than the average of all juveniles arrested.

CHAPTER FIVE

DELINQUENCY AND HOMES

Family Settings

There were 326 broken homes in all. The father was dead in 81; the mother was dead in 51. In 38, the parents were divorced and in 102 they were separated, while the father had deserted 54 others. This is the count of homes at the time of their first break; in 74, a second disruption occurred prior to the boy's first delinquent act. In most such cases, the change was from desertion or separation to divorce, although other sequences were found.

Careful consideration showed that the more recent condition was the one with the greatest meaning to the child. The following illustration is typical of the situation. The father left his home and wandered west. The children were deeply agitated by his departure and always believed that he would soon come back to them and their mother. While he was away, he became ill and died. The youngsters were grief-stricken. It was not the shame of the separation, but the loss of their parent that grieved them. There were other cases like this with breaks of typologically inconsistent kinds. There were also 22 which began in one of the pre-selected categories and later fell into an outside class; for example, the death of a parent was followed by a step-parent deserting the family. These were retained as a separate group.

In the final distribution, there were 81 families in which the father was dead; in 53 the mother had died; in 65 the parents were divorced, and in 71, they had separated. In 34 families, the father deserted, and in another 22, there were other conditions. Appendix C shows in detail the relations of first breaks to family status at the time of delinquency.

Delinquent Acts

At least three definitions might be given for the object of study, the first offense. Which shall be chosen: (1) First sign of delinquency, official or not, as judged in retrospect from the boy's record? (2) First apprehension by the police? (3) First adjudication of delinquency in court?

The use of first adjudication was discussed in Chapter II, where it was shown that it often does not represent the first delinquency. The Gluecks found a wide difference between the age at first appearance and the age at onset of delinquency. Of five hundred delinquents, four appeared in court prior to eight years of age, while by this same age, 242 had shown definite signs of misbehavior, judged by a review of their records.[1] There may be a long lapse between the beginning of misbehavior and the first misbehavior judged in court, and during this time many changes in the family could occur.

A retrospective review involves a different type of temporal error. It is difficult to determine the date of delinquency onset when the naming of the first such act depends on subjective judgment. Knowledge of later behavior or of family events may affect the labeling of earlier acts which might otherwise have been considered within socially tolerable limits. The best available criterion for distinguishing the first delinquent act is arrest by the police. Of the three alternatives, this is the most free from selectional and subjective bias. The possibilities of error in police judgment were examined in Chapter II; they are smaller in magnitude than those introduced by the other two standards.

Offenses must be divided between the "less" and the "more" serious. Scales for grading delinquencies have been prepared by Slawson,[2] Clark,[3] Durea,[4] and Powers and Witmer.[5] Slawson, as mentioned before, built his scale largely on the number of days of imprisonment or dollar fines an adult might receive for a given act. The rest were based on ratings by correctional workers and other people. These lists were examined, and offenses committed by juveniles before the Mercer County Court and others were reviewed. A scale was then prepared, shown below, reflecting the acts of the boys actually studied. This scale differentiates groups of offenses but not offenses within the groups, for random events too often set apart grand and petty larceny, and the rounds of the police may stop a forced entry from becoming a burglary, for example. These differences therefore represent variations in outside events, not behavioral distinctions.

MINOR OFFENSES

1. Discipline problems: malicious mischief, truancy, incorrigibility, false alarm, running away, disorderly conduct, indecent language, trespassing
2. Assault
3. Motor vehicle violations (Note: not included in this study)
4. Fornication

SERIOUS OFFENSES

5. Larceny: petty larceny, larceny, grand larceny; selling lottery tickets; taking auto without owner's consent; receiving stolen goods
6. Burglary: breaking and entry; entry and larceny; breaking, entry and larceny
7. Carrying concealed weapons
8. Serious sex offenses: carnal abuse; fellatio; indecent exposure. (No cases of rape found in this study)
9. Atrocious assault and battery
10. Arson
11. Robbery

The classification was submitted to the juvenile officers at the Trenton Court for their review. They proposed no changes. Durea suggests that duration and frequency of misbehavior should be considered.[6] These factors do not apply to this study, which included only first offenders.

The distribution of offenses appears in Appendix D. Some boys shown there committed several infractions each in the escapades leading to arrest, such as truanting and burglarizing a house. The more serious act was considered his in such a case.

The scale was applied to divide delinquents into two classes; those committing serious and those committing minor offenses.[7] This division was used in family comparisons, which were based on ratios of serious offenses among boys in family groups.

Statistical Operations

By what method are proportions of serious offenses of boys in any two family classifications to be compared? The most important fact is that all boys, whatever their homes, were delinquent; they formed a single universe. Therefore, family classification or sub-groups should be compared not to each other but to the group as a whole.

The percentage of serious acts for the entire group, or universe, was 63.3. Subgroup percentages were tested by asking: Could the criterion percentage of 63.3 have varied this far by chance alone, if based on the number of cases in the subgroup being considered? This is expressed in the formula for the critical ratio:

$$\frac{P_t - P_s}{\sqrt{\dfrac{P_t \times Q_t}{N_s}}}$$

where P_t and Q_t were p and q for the universe, or 63.3 per cent and 36.7 per cent; P_s was p for the subgroup; and N_s was the actual number of cases in the subgroup; where N_s included unbroken homes, only those contained in the 25 per cent sample of all unbroken homes were counted in.[8]

The fact of sampling required consideration of the manner of selecting the criterion percentage, which was taken to represent the proportion of serious offenses in the universe. When unbroken homes were weighted by four to represent their share of all 1,050 cases reviewed, serious offenses were 63.3 per cent; when only the 181 unbroken recorded were added, serious offenses were 61.3 per cent. The two hardly differed, but the first better balanced the family types and was considered closer to the actual parameter value.

In testing variations from the criterion through use of critical ratios, a confidence limit of 5 per cent, or 1.96 standard errors, was used throughout this report. Wherever it is said that a percentage is "significant" it means that the variation was this much or more. Exceptions are explained when they occur.

Crucial Tests

The most important question can now be tested: do boys from broken homes commit a less than average proportion of serious delinquencies? Of those from unbroken homes, 65.2 per cent of the acts were serious. For boys from broken homes, the figure was 59.2 per cent. This appears to prove that minor offenses are indeed associated with family disruptions. However, neither proportion, unbroken or broken, differs significantly from 63.3 per cent. The difference for broken homes is 4.1 per cent ± 2.7 per cent and for the unbroken, 1.9 per cent ± 3.6 per cent; the null hypothesis therefore applies.

There were 139 boys with special family situations not

included in this study, comprising, as explained in Chapter Four, fifty-five illegitimate or adopted boys and eighty-four with family situations excluded from consideration. A quarter of these was sampled, and it was found that 61.3 per cent of their acts were serious. Therefore, what has been found applies to them as well as to other boys from broken homes.

The second vital question is now to be considered. Among the boys from broken homes, is the percentage of serious acts lowest for those whose homes were broken by desertion, separation, or divorce? This group is to be contrasted to those who lost a parent through death. When boys are classed by their status at delinquency, the percentage for orphans was 57.5 and for others, 58.8. Classed by first break, the figures are for the boys, 58.3 and 59.8. Neither of these represents a significant difference from 63.3 per cent.

Reference again is made to Appendix C. Among the seventy-four twice broken homes, the serious infractions were 60.8 per cent. This is not a significant variation. The same applies to the twenty-two "other" cases, starting in one of the categories and ending outside of them. Their percentage was 72.7, not significant in a group their size. Similar conclusions apply to the inconsistent cases in which death followed divorce or divorce of step-parent followed death. In summation, type of break was not associated with behavior in a significantly discernible manner.

Do boys from broken and unbroken homes commit different sorts of offenses? A full display of delinquencies according to family situations is given in Appendix D. These data may be and were analyzed by the same methods as those applied to "serious" and "minor" percentages, explained above in detail. It was found, in fact, that truancy was significantly more common and petty larceny significantly rarer among the broken home boys. The maximum percentage of truancy for these boys allowable by a 5 per cent confidence limit would have been 5.5, while the observed percentage was 6.4.

For petty larceny, the minimum allowable percentage would have been 13.6, while it was actually 12.9. These discrepancies are small and they do not appear to invalidate the general conclusion that broken and unbroken homes do not differ significantly in their effects on delinquent behavior.

CHAPTER SIX

THE RESULTS OF INEQUALITIES

"Comparisouns doon offte gret greuaunce," said Lydgate in the year of 1430. Today we know well that research and knowledge depend on comparisons, if these are made under correct and equal conditions. Yet, what if in our research we contrast two family groups which are dissimilar in some vital respect?

Let us anticipate material which appears later in this chapter. For boys of divorce, the percentage of serious offenses was 55.4, not significantly low. A certain portion of them had a seriousness rate of only 46.2 per cent; these were youths supervised in their free time by their mothers or substitute mothers. But this part of the group was proportionately smaller in size than among the delinquents at large: two-fifths as opposed to five-eighths. What if five-eighths of the boys with divorced parents had been supervised in this way and if the extent of each other mode of care had also been precisely the same as among all the delinquents? The answer is given by weighting the percentages of serious acts in the supervisional categories of the subgroups in divorce by the percentages of total cases in equivalent cells. In the table on the following page, this figure, or corrected percentage, is .680 × 46.2, plus .066 × 40.0, plus .254 × 66.7, or 50.5 per cent.[1] This differs significantly from the total rate of 63.3 per cent.

TABLE 4

SUPERVISION AMONG BOYS OF DIVORCE

	All Cases	Divorce Cases
Mother or substitute supervised		
Serious offenses	63.0%	46.2%
Proportion of cases	.680	.400
Poor supervision		
Serious offenses	49.3%	40.0%
Proportion of cases	.066	.092
Other supervision		
Serious offenses	67.8%	66.7%
Proportion of cases	.254	.508
Total		
Serious offenses	63.3%	55.4%
Proportion of cases	1.000	1.000

What has been explained herein was applied to all family percentages for twenty-one groups of controls.[2] These were variables which in themselves might have been causes of delinquency, or have influenced its mode of expression, or have affected the observation or reporting of delinquent behavior. Not all writers agree on the meanings of factors employed as controls. Some, for example, say that a high rate of delinquency in a given locale engenders more delinquency there. Others say that high rates are the results of selective migration, while still others would point to the differential enforcement of law. Whichever position is truest, there is a need, it seems, to correct for rates of delinquency in the areas in which the contrasted cases resided.

Variables in this study applied as controls were all those on which consistent material of a reasonably objective nature could be obtained from the case records.

A Word on Restricted Selection

Cases included neither Negroes nor girls; white boys alone were studied and this resembles control of the factors of sex and of race. Delinquency rates and sex are associated. In Newark, New Jersey, in the year ending in August of 1955, for example, of 2,184 juvenile court appearances, only 392 were girls.[3] Girls, more often than boys, may express anti-social feelings in ways that are not delinquent. Girls are in general more closely supervised than are boys, while the police may be lenient toward them, especially for minor offenses. A girl's reaction to a break in the home may be more severe than that of a boy.[4] These differences demand control of sex in comparisons; yet the number of girls before the juvenile court in Trenton in 1957, for instance, was only sixty-seven of a total of 410 cases.[5] This portion is too small for an adequate study of girls as a group.

Boys are the larger group, and the larger part of the boys are white, more than 60 per cent of cases in 1957.[6] The Negroes, who were smaller in numbers, require experimental control as a group: Negroes are treated differently from whites by police, as Sellin[7] and Castendyck and Robison[8] have shown. The reactions of the juvenile Negroes to breaks in their homes may differ from those of whites, especially if families have recently come from the South. Frazier[9] has portrayed the characteristics of this type of family; the departure of father from the home where the mother is the dominant figure has an impact differing vastly from the departure of the father from another family.

Controls of Consequence

All broken home seriousness rates differed by less variation than 5 per cent chance from the over-all percentage of 63.3, but correction by three controls each caused one broken home percentage to become significant.

INTELLIGENCE Theories, which are reviewed by Phelps, for example, have been posed to explain delinquency as the product of low intelligence.[10] It has also been proposed, as suggested by McCord and McCord, that boys with higher intelligence are more clever in escaping arrest.[11]

A four-part division of cases by mental ability was used: normal and above (I.Q., 90 and over); dull normal (I.Q., 80-89); borderline (I.Q., 68-79); moron and below (I.Q., under 67). These groupings reflect current clinical practices. Where a rating was not based on a test, but upon evaluation by a correctional worker, the verbal classification matching this judgment was used.[12]

The effect of correction by intelligence group was to lower one rate to a significant level—that for boys of divorce became 50.7 per cent.[13]

TABLE 5

INTELLIGENCE OF BOYS

	Number	Serious Offenses
Normal intelligence	588	66.8%
Dull normal	205	59.0%
Borderline	143	60.1%
Moron and below	114	57.0%

There was no significant relation between delinquent behavior and the intelligence of the boys, as such.

SUPERVISION The importance of this factor was discovered at the beginning of the chapter, but additional remarks are needed. Attention to this matter began with concern for the effects on children of the employment of mothers. Many children whose mothers work no doubt suffer from lack of affection or the inability of their mothers to give it. But it was found that the situation is not a simple one. In some unbroken homes, the children received no maternal attention, but were left in charge of school-age sisters, even though the mothers were not employed. In others, the mothers were ill and could not care for their families. No relation was found between working mothers and the behavior of boys, as shown in the table below. Because of this finding, the matter was approached from another direction.

TABLE 6A

WORKING MOTHERS*

	Number	*Serious offenses*
Did not work	688	62.1%
Mother and father both worked	250	67.6%
Mother worked; father unemployed	24	66.7%
Mother worked; was head of home	48	54.2%
No mother figure in the home	40	67.5%

* Mothers or mother figures here include grandmothers, etc.; this table differs slightly from others in which only mothers are counted.

The real question about the boys was this: who got them off to school, minded them when they came home after classes and after supper until they went to bed, and saw that they kept out of trouble in their other free hours?

One ten-year-old was under the care of this thirteen-year-old sister, from whom the police learned of his misbehavior. The mother of another boy worked as a cashier and usually sent her young son to the diner for supper and then to a movie until ten or eleven o'clock. If he wished, he would run to his brother's home or go where he would. In another home, the mother ran a store under the family home, and it was her son's role to keep out of the way while she worked. Conditions like these furnish poor supervision and, as a form of weak control, were found to be associated with a significantly large proportion of minor offenses; the seriousness rate for boys of this kind was 49.3 per cent.

The table which follows shows the supervisional situations in detail. Mother figures in this table include stepmothers, foster mothers, and grandmothers. A small group of ill fathers who stayed at home all the time while the mothers worked are also included with "mother figures in the home." Correction for supervisional situation reduced the proportion of serious offenses in homes broken by divorce to 50.1 per cent, a level that was significantly low.

TABLE 6B

How Boys Were Supervised*

	Number	Serious Offenses
Mother figure in the home	714	63.0%
No care after school and at night	39	51.3%
Parent worked at home	15	53.3%
By another sibling who was in school	15	40.0%
Total	69	49.3%
No care after school until supper	117	61.5%
By a non-family adult	8	75.0%
By a sibling 16-17 not in school	9	100.0%
By other family member	67	67.2%
Parent worked during school hours	17	70.6%
Parents worked different shifts	36	69.4%
Boy worked day; with parents evenings	13	92.3%
Total	267	67.8%

* Corrected percentages shown in Appendix F are based upon the categories shown here.

The Results of Inequalities

CALENDAR PERIOD   Seriousness rates varied by year, reflecting changes in correctional policies and social trends affecting delinquent behavior. Two aspects of the former are to be particularly noted. The rate for the span 1937, 1938, and 1939 was especially and significantly high. Most of the cases studied came through the Bureau of Juvenile Aid of the Department of Police of the City of Trenton. The Bureau began in 1937, and available information indicates that its policies during the early years were different from those later pursued. In the former period, the Bureau was viewed more strictly as a police agency, and for the most part only those boys needing correctional treatment were referred to Court. Later, those felt to be in need of guidance were sent in greater proportion. In addition, the juvenile court age was changed in 1948, raising the limit from the seventeenth birthday to the nineteenth. The rate for the period 1950-54 was significantly low, perhaps reflecting the age-limit policy change. Correction for time period lowered the rate for boys whose homes were broken by divorce to a significant level, which was 50.9 per cent.[14]

TABLE 7

CALENDAR PERIOD

	Number	Serious Offenses
1937 - 1939	180	83.3%
1940 - 1944	262	64.1%
1945 - 1949	246	62.2%
1950 - 1954	246	50.0%
1955 - 1959	116	61.2%

The divorce group rate—and this rate only—was significantly altered by correction for three controls: intelligence, supervision, and calendar period. What these effects mean will be judged when all the evidence has been considered.

The Controls and Delinquency

Significant linkage to delinquent behavior was found in two of the controls which have been described: negative linkage to poor home supervision and the calendar period 1950-54, and positive to the period 1937-39. Other conditions were also found to have such traits. None of these others affected the seriousness rates of family groups when applied as corrections, but all were associated beyond chance expectation with degree of delinquent behavior.

SOCIAL STATUS Sutherland and Cressey state that "if two persons of different economic levels are equally guilty of the same offense, the one of the lower level is more likely to be arrested, convicted and committed to an institution."[15] Robison voices conclusions of similar kind.[16] Involved here are the socio-economic statuses of the boys in this study. These may be estimated by income, ratings of prestige, home ownership, or occupation of the head of the home. Nineteen such criteria were examined by Kahl and Davis.[17] Occupation, as divided by census classifications and Warner's scale, were found by factor analyses of tetrachoric correlations to be the most reliable indicators of status.

Occupational classes of the chief wage earners in homes were used in this study, based on the divisions created by the U. S. Bureau of the Census.[18] These groups were established: (1) professional, technical, and kindred workers; managers, officials, and proprietors; (2) clerical and kindred workers, sales workers; (3) craftsmen, foremen, and kindred workers; (4) operators and kindred workers; (5) service workers, except household; (6) laborers, and other service workers, including household; (7) unemployed. If the person had had his occupation changed, his present class was used, and if he held several jobs, his main one was used. Those out of work over six months receiving financial aid or those never regularly employed were classed as unemployed.

TABLE 8

Chief Wage Earners' Occupations*

	Number	Serious Offenses
Professional and Clerical	124	50.8%
Foremen and Craftsmen	213	61.5%
Operators	330	69.4%
Service and Unskilled	307	63.2%
Unemployed	76	63.2%

* The seven groups given in the text were combined to make five in tabulations and corrections.

The seriousness rate for boys of white-collar families was significantly low. Further analysis proved this to be a spurious correlation. There were only fourteen white-collar cases during 1937, 1938, and 1939. When these were removed, the professional-clerical rate was 51.8 per cent, which did not significantly differ from the criterion of 63.3 per cent.[19]

RELIEF AND AID TO THE FAMILY Some families received some or all of their income from outside. This came from relatives, children, or organized aid. It should be expected that economic deprivation and the confusion of roles resulting from outside help would disorganize the family and weaken solidarity and control. There should be a smaller proportion of serious offenses in boys from such homes. The opposite of this anticipation was found. Relief was associated with serious, not minor offenses.

The unexpected result was the effect of a spurious correlation. The period of 1937 through 1939 contained a high concentration of families receiving aid. When cases receiving aid were corrected for the distribution of calendar period, their percentage of serious offenses dropped to the nonsignificant level of 67.4 per cent.

TABLE 9

RELIEF AND AID TO THE FAMILY

	Number	Serious Offenses
Relatives supported	6	66.7%
Relatives helped	12	50.0%
Children helped	70	77.1%
Total*	88	72.7%
General Assistance	40	82.5%
Aid to Dependent Children	19	57.9%
General Assistance, and help from children	24	58.3%
Other combination	15	86.7%
Total*	98	72.4%
Pension, etc.	18	61.1%
Unemployment Compensation	9	100.0%
W.P.A.	43	72.1%
Total*	70	72.9%
Total for any kind of aid	256	72.7%
No aid of any kind*	794	60.3%

* Corrected percentages based on distributions by these totals.

NEUROTIC BOYS Delinquency has often been ascribed to the effects of mental disturbances and therefore note was made of such indications in the recorded histories of the boys, as reflected in school transcripts, special examinations, and field investigations. Three categories of mental condition were developed: normal or no difficulty reported; psychotic or brain damage; and neurotic. This last included cases diagnosed by psychiatrists, and also stutterers, non-readers and similar individuals.

Neurotic disturbances were associated with a very significantly low rate of serious offenses.

TABLE 10

MENTAL PROBLEMS OF BOYS

	Number	Serious Offenses
Normal or no difficulty reported	916	67.4%
Psychotic or brain damage	31	51.6%
Neurotic, stutterers, etc.	103	31.1%

DISABLED MOTHERS   A mother, a father, or a sibling with a mental abnormality is a most disturbing influence in the family. One boy told of seeing his father, who was a psychotic, return home late at night and urinate upon the floor. The strains to which the families of the mentally ill are subjected are described by Clausen and Yarrow.[20] Physical disabilities also cause strain. If the father is an invalid, if the mother is diabetic or crippled, if there is a bedridden grandmother in the house, there are unusual problems to work out.

These were the findings for mothers:[21]

TABLE 11

DISABILITIES OF MOTHER FIGURES

	Number	Serious Offenses
Total number of boys with a mother figure at home	1,019	63.3%
Mother figure normal	836	61.2%
Mother figure mentally abnormal	84	56.0%
Mother figure physically disabled or ill	99	86.9%

Mental abnormality included excessive drinking, alcoholism, instability, psychosis, and mental defect. Physical disability included illness; being crippled, invalid, or disabled; or being disfigured. The percentage of serious offenses was significantly high among boys with physically disabled mothers. A similar trend, though never of significant proportions, was observed in boys who witnessed physical disabilities among (1) father figures when these were at home, (2) supervisors, (3) siblings, and (4) household members not part of the family.

The association of mothers' handicaps and behavior was not influenced by correction for receipt of relief or year of arrest of the boy.[22]

RELIGIOUS CONFLICT   In the majority of cases, both of each boy's parents were of the same faith: Catholic, Jewish, or Protestant, whether he lived with his original parents or with

TABLE 12

RELIGIOUS CONFLICT OF PARENTS†

	Number	Serious Offenses
Home unbroken		
Parents' religions the same	644	68.3%
Parents' religions differed	80	40.0%
Home broken within last two years; no step-parents		
Parents' religions the same	48	68.7%
Parents' religions differed	10	40.0%
Home broken over two years ago; no step-parents		
Parents' religions the same	119	60.4%
Parents' religions differed	26	61.5%
With step- or foster parents		
Parents' religions the same*	107	54.2%
Parents' religions differed*	16	62.5%

† When faith of a parent was unknown, it was assumed to be the same as that of the known parent.
* Natural parent and step-parent, or foster parents, compared.

a step- and a natural parent. Where faiths differed, conflict was possible, leading to demoralization, reduction of social control, and a lower rate of serious offenses. This is made clear when we separate boys with unbroken homes and those whose homes were recently broken and who had no step-parent. For these two groups where religious affiliations clashed, the seriousness rate was low and significant, 40.0 per cent.

FOREIGN-BORN PARENTS There are many enclaves or settlements of the foreign-born and those of foreign extraction in Trenton. Italians, Poles, and others have well-defined areas within the city. It should be expected that in such locales there would be resistance to assimilation, reflected in stricter control of the boys, and that the offenses of boys in such settings should be more serious, in the main; this was in fact found to be true, when both parents were born abroad.[23]

TABLE 13

FOREIGN-BORN PARENTS

	Number	Serious Offenses
Boy with one or both parents; no step-parents		
Neither foreign-born	618	59.9%
Mother foreign-born	45	71.1%
Father foreign-born	105	61.1%
Both foreign-born	179	79.9%
Boy with parent (and step-parent)	103	54.4%

AGE CLUSTERS Of all boys, only certain ones undergo conditions which can produce delinquent behavior. These conditions, internal or external, can arise at different ages, and the older the youth, the more serious the delinquent behavior produced is likely to be; most of the younger boys have not the strength or the skill to commit burglary or armed robbery, while any pupil can truant or can maliciously break a school window.

Also, the proportion of homes broken is a function of age. There were in this study 23.8 per cent disrupted families among boys through the age of twelve; among those over that age, 37.0 per cent. For this reason it was important to see if correction for age affected family group rates. It did not; however, relations of age in itself to behavior were discovered:

TABLE 14

AGE AT FIRST KNOWN OFFENSE

	Number	Serious Offenses
4-10 years old	228	47.4%
11 or 12 years old	244	73.8%
13-15 years old	454	61.7%
16 or 17 years old	124	78.3%

All of these but the thirteen-to-fifteen-year-old group differed significantly from the total per cent of 63.3.

PROTESTANT PIETY Religion was used as a control for the differences it might involve in the effects on the boy of a broken home and for possible differences in attitudes on the part of correctional authorities toward various groups; this has been discussed by Robison.[24] Cases were separated into Catholic, Jewish, and Protestant groups; Catholic included Greek Orthodox. Devoutness was gauged by regularity of attendance at church or interest in religious affairs, as reported by the Probation Department.

Among Protestant boys, a significantly high proportion of serious offenses was found among the devout; among the non-devout it was significantly low. These relations did not appear among Catholic or Jewish cases.

TABLE 15

RELIGIOUS AFFILIATION AND INTEREST OF BOY

		Number	*Serious Offenses*
Protestant	Devout	104	77.9%
	Not Devout	223	53.4%
	Unknown	9	88.9%
Catholic	Devout	388	63.9%
	Not Devout	284	67.6%
	Unknown	21	71.4%
Jewish	Devout	5	20.0%
	Not devout	16	6.3%
	Unknown	0	0.0%

There is here a group of factors associated with the seriousness of delinquent behavior: home supervision, calendar period, neuroticism, disability of mothers, religious conflict of parents, foreign birth of parents, age at first delinquency, and the boys' religious behavior.[25]

Factors with No Effect

WHAT KIND OF NEIGHBORHOOD?–"BAD AREAS" Thrasher and Shaw have delineated the "special dangers of rearing children in high delinquency areas," says Barnes.[26] In such sections, near the homes of boys, often there are *bolita*-men, convicts, and prostitutes. One investigator advised the Court concerning a boy from such a place, "Don't make a hero of him by giving him probation—just dismiss the charges."

To assess these dangers, delinquency rates were prepared by year and ward[27] of the city. Arrest figures by ward were supplied by the Trenton Bureau of Juvenile Aid for the years 1941 through 1959; figures for 1937, 1938, 1939, and 1940 were prepared from lists of Bureau cases preserved in the files of the Court. Population figures of wards were obtained from the U. S. Census reports for 1930[28] and 1940.[29] Figures by ward and by age were not published for 1950, but the Census Bureau supplied a special tabulation for this study.[30]

Population figures for 1960 were not available when the data were analyzed. Full and sample counts were made of all juveniles aged five to fifteen, represented by kindergarten through ninth-grade enrollments, in schools in Trenton in 1958-59. This count was made in cooperation with the Trenton Public School System, the Trenton Diocese of the Roman Catholic Church, and the Jewish Federation of Trenton.

The school span of ages five to fifteen and not the delinquent span of five to seventeen was used for enumeration: Youths may drop out of school at sixteen in the State of New Jersey, thus reducing their numbers in the rolls. However, for 1930, 1940, and 1950, the five to fifteen year old group was found to be a reasonably constant proportion of ages 5-17. The former comprised of the latter 76.5 per cent, 72.0 per cent, and 77.6 per cent in these years, respectively.

Populations for years intervening were arithmetically or logarithmically interpolated. In computing delinquency rates for each ward-year, a moving average was used, based upon the arrests for the current and two prior years, which was done to smooth out excessive annual fluctuations, divided by the population of the year involved. The same set of rates was used for the first years, 1937, 1938, 1939, and 1940.

To determine the statistical significance of rates, the method explained in Chapter Five was used; it was determined whether the ward rate for a given year differed significantly from that for all the wards combined for that year.[31] Three classes were denoted: significantly under the average; significantly above the average; and average.

Boys in this study were classed by the rates of their wards

of residence at the time they became delinquent. The result was a finding that there was no significant relation between neighborhood (or ward) delinquency rates and the boys' behavior.

TABLE 16

BOYS CLASSIFIED BY DELINQUENCY RATES OF WARDS
OF RESIDENCE

	Number	Serious Offenses
Below average	445	61.8%
Above average	473	64.9%
Average	132	62.9%

Additional analyses were made. There was found to be no relation between delinquency rate and behavior, when consideration was given to length of residence in the area or to the type of area in which the boy had previously lived. It was also found that there was no connection between immediate and later referral to court (this is discussed later in more detail) and area. In good, bad, and average areas the percentages of boys referred to court at once were 55.7, 44.8, and 53.1, none of which differed significantly from the total percentage of 50.5 immediate referrals. In other words, correctional treatment was not related to area. One obvious connection to area was found. The average population for below average rate ward-years was 1,519; 445 study cases came from such areas; for above average, the figures were 936 and 473; for average, 741 and 132. This shows that more cases came from the areas with the higher delinquency rates.

The study by Shaw and McKay was reviewed in earlier pages; mention was made of their failure to consider the possible travel of students to schools outside of their locales. Does this relate to this study? Cases were divided between those up to twelve, mostly in nearby schools (not always in the same ward) and those over twelve who might travel away from home. Upon this division, one relation was found. Boys under twelve in good areas had a seriousness rate of 50.00 per cent ($N = 192$; $N_s = 84$), which differs significantly from the total rate for those under twelve, 61.02 per cent; however, the lower 5 per cent confidence limit for 61.02 per cent with N_s 84 is 50.58 per cent. A difference of 0.58 per cent is inadequate support for conclusions which depart from those previously stated.

Mowrer suggests that "delinquency areas" are the product of differential migration or similar forces.[32] This explanation seems possible in the absence of observable connections between the rates of the areas themselves and the boys' behavior. It appears at the least that the state of the neighborhood is not related to individual deportment. Robison holds that discrepancies in the enforcement of law may also produce apparent high rates of delinquency in certain parts of the city.[33] This does not appear to be so, in view of the results above cited on the proportion of immediate as compared to later referrals to court. In addition, when calendar period was reviewed, no relation between area and the particular high-rate period 1937-39 was discovered. The percentages of serious offenses among boys from good, bad, and indifferent areas for that period were 82.6, 85.0 and 82.3; for 1940-59 they were 59.4, 59.5, and 56.2. Correctional policy, by time, was not related to the seriousness rates by area.

WHAT KIND OF NEIGHBORHOOD?–"BAD GANGS" Boys often commit their offenses in association with others, and this is presumptive evidence that gang membership is a causative factor in delinquency. Shaw and McKay found that only 18.2 per cent of their boys committed their offenses alone; 30.3 per cent shared the act with one other boy; 27.7 per cent with two; 10.8 per cent with three; and 13.0 per cent with four and over.[34] The Gluecks declare that such results prove only that "birds of a feather flock together";[35] yet if this be so, no information should be lost in examining the subject.

In the records of the boys in this study the names of others involved in the act were mentioned. It did not prove possible to construct a picture of gangs from this material, but the presence or absence of associates was studied. It was found that three offenses were, by their nature, usually committed alone: running away, truancy, and incorrigibility. Only 18 of 114 boys committed these acts in the company of associates. When running away, etc., were excluded, the total percentage of serious offenses was 71.0; for lone offenders it was 61.2, and for those with one or more companions, 73.2; neither of these differs by less than 5 per cent chance from 71.0 per cent.

TABLE 17

COMPANIONS IN THE OFFENSE

(*Running Away, Truancy, Incorrigibility Excluded*)

	Number	Serious Offenses
Lone Offenses	165	61.2%
One or More Companions	771	73.2%
Total, Running away, etc. excluded	936	71.0%

Correction was made in the unbroken-broken home rates for the actual number of accomplices. There were no changes in seriousness rates (see Appendix F). Lenroot has suggested that gang membership may be more important for boys from unbroken homes, since the boy from the broken home is propelled toward delinquency by the rupture itself.[36] This conclusion is not supported by the results in Chapter Five, nor by those just cited. Also relevant here are the comparative seriousness rates for boys with no accomplices. For those with unbroken homes, the rate was 38.1 per cent and for the broken, 39.8 per cent. This does not reflect any independent effect of the break on behavior.

WORKING BOYS The juveniles on whom this book is based included many who worked as errand boys, newsboys, shoeshiners, and at summer jobs. Some of the older ones held regular positions. Street jobs and premature adult contacts, Barnes and Teeters say,[37] throw a boy into poor company and may increase the likelihood of his becoming delinquent. The findings are these:

TABLE 18

EMPLOYMENT OF BOYS

	Number	Serious Offenses
In school, did not work	765	60.4%
In school, part-time work	215	68.4%
Out of school, unemployed	23	73.9%
Out of school, employed	47	83.0%

The rate for those not in school and employed was significantly high, but this group was composed of boys sixteen and seventeen years of age, whose rate was 78.3 per cent; 83.0 per cent does not differ by less than 5 per cent chance from this. Further, when all cases were divided between those under and over thirteen, no relation of delinquency and employment was found in the created groups.

MOVING FROM PLACE TO PLACE What happens to a boy if he is moved from neighborhood to neighborhood? Mobile families have special attributes; Schorr[38] and VanValen[39] have found that marriages in this kind of family have unusual solidarity, but that parents and children are not adjusted to their host communities. The effects of these factors were considered. Three groups were denoted: no moves in two years; one move in two years; and two moves in two years. It was believed that after two years a boy could be considered a part of his neighborhood.

TABLE 19

Moves of Boy's Household

	Number	Serious Offenses
No moves in two years	851	63.3%
One move in two years	133	58.6%
Two or moves in two years	66	72.7%

None of the figures in Table 19 is significant. The possibility was probed that the nature of a boy's present neighborhood might have altered the effect of mobility. Delinquency rates for areas of residence were cross-tabulated with mobility; the seriousness rate in no one of the cells was significant.

DISCRIMINATION BY FAMILY SITUATION If a policeman sees two boys he knows, each committing the same offense, and one is from a broken home, would he sooner arrest this lad than the other and sooner send him to court? If this were a fact about the cases composing this study, it would certainly have inflated the numbers of boys from broken homes with minor offenses. The possibility of this sort of bias was investigated. Cases were divided between those referred to court for the first time for their first known offenses, and those referred to court for the first time for later offenses. In this analysis boys were excluded whose families had changed between first offense and original referral to court; twelve boys from originally unbroken homes were dropped, as were four from originally broken homes who later experienced still another break.

Of the 1,034 cases, 51.3 per cent were referred at once with 72.3 per cent serious offenses. Of those referred later, 70.2 per cent of the offenses for which they were petitioned to court were serious. No family subgroup proportion differed significantly from these over-all figures. At first court appearance, all boys were approximately fourteen years in median age. For those sent at once, the median among the boys from unbroken homes was 13.85 years, while for those from broken homes it was 14.27. The former differs significantly from the over-all median age at referral of 14.23 years, but the actual disparity in age between unbroken and broken was only four months and a half. For those sent later, the unbroken median was 14.47 years, and the broken, 14.35. Broken home subgroups within the immediate and later referral groups were tested against the total median age at referral. Boys of separated parents referred for their first offenses were significantly younger than others; their median age was 13.08 $\pm$ .53 years.

Average arrests were computed by counting all apprehensions from the first through the ones for which the boys were finally sent to court, among the boys not sent at once. The average for all was 2.98. One subgroup differed significantly; boys with father dead had 2.47 $\pm$ .18 arrests.

All groups had about the same proportion of immediate referrals, the same proportions of serious offenses at first appearance in court, the same median age at appearance, and the same average number of arrests. The exceptions did not overlap any one group of cases and the results appear to apply to all. This permits an important generalization: readiness for referral to juvenile court was a definite status, designated without regard to family condition and defined by age and behavior.

Other potentials for bias were inspected. It has been said already that the change in Juvenile Court age in 1948 did not affect seriousness rates. However, in order to compensate for the change in age, all sixteen- and seventeen-year-olds who appeared in the Probation Office files prior to 1948 under other court jurisdictions were used in this study though they were not then legally juveniles. There were thirty-five of these (N_s 20). It may also be mentioned that prior to 1943, some cases were "unofficially" handled. These were boys for whom it was wished to avoid court processing. There were fourteen of these (N_s 8). These inclusions made no material difference to family group rates when correction for them was made.

BROTHERS AND SISTERS The effects of family size and ordinal position upon the child have been discussed by many writers. Woofter discusses the relation of size and income;[40] Wattenburg analyzes the delinquency of the only child.[41] A general review of the relationships of siblings and delinquency is given by Sutherland and Cressey.[42]

There were in this study ninety boys who had step-brothers or sisters, including twenty-eight boys from unbroken homes, one of whose parents had been married before. The seriousness rate of the group was 58.9%, not significantly low. Because of this lack of effect, all siblings were combined in analyses here, and for other reasons besides. Many cases were found in which there were true bonds of affection between boys and their step-brothers or sisters; in other instances there were no ties between boys and true siblings. Also combined were all brothers and sisters whether in or out of the home; it was not only to those at home that the boy compared himself.

The number of siblings was not related in any significant way to delinquent behavior, except for only children in unbroken homes.

TABLE 20

NUMBER OF SIBLINGS
(*Including the Boy Himself*)

	Number	Serious Offenses
Only child	54	46.3%
Two to four	550	63.3%
Five to seven	285	64.6%
Eight or more	161	67.1%

The rate for only children was based on twenty-four unbroken homes, in which the rate was 16.7 per cent, and thirty broken, with a rate of 70.0 per cent. N_s for the unbroken was six, and 16.7 per cent is significant even for this small a group. Where $p = 0.633$, and $N = 6$, the binomial probability for $K = 1$ is 2.529 per cent, and for $K = 0$, 0.243 per cent, or a total of 2.772 per cent.

Ordinal position had no effect on family rates, nor any relation to delinquent behavior. Relative position was also considered; this is a refinement of ordinal classification. To be the second of two siblings is not the same as to be the second of five, nor the fourth of four the same as the fourth of nine. The categories only child, first of two, second of two, first of three or more, and so on were established. These were not related to delinquent behavior nor did they affect family rates.

FAMILY DELINQUENCY There appears to be evidence that juvenile misbehavior is associated with delinquency among siblings. Healy and Bronner[43] found that 78 per cent of delinquent children in two-child families had delinquent siblings; the figure, by contrast, in six-child families was 43 per cent. The Gluecks also found a much higher proportion of delinquents than non-delinquents with delinquent or criminal mothers, fathers, and siblings.[44]

Information on the delinquent and criminal behavior of family members was available from two sources in the Court: descriptions in the boys' own files and in separate files of the household members themselves. Both these sources were fully reviewed, but no attempt was made to secure reports from the Police Department or authorities outside of Trenton.

Offenses of mothers, fathers, siblings, and anyone, including these persons or others, in the family or household were compared to the seriousness rates of the boys. Distinction was made among non-offenders, single offenders, and recidivists, and for parents, whether they were with the boy or not. As control factors, these records of relatives did not affect any of the seriousness rates of the family groups. There was some indication that family recidivism itself was associated with minor offenses by boys. Among ninety-four with single offender fathers, the rate was 72.3 per cent; among ninety-six with recidivist fathers, 50.0 per cent. Similar figures for siblings were ninety-seven, 66.0 per cent and 237, 57.0 per cent respectively; for all in the family or household taken together, 162, 67.9 per cent and 371, 60.6 per cent; for mothers, 28, 25.0 per cent, 46, 63.0 per cent. None of these figures differed significantly from 63.3 per cent, the total proportion. However, they formed a pattern, except for the mothers, which suggests that family control of the boys was tightened after a member went astray, but became weakened under repeated infractions of law.

It was believed that more visible effect might be obtained if recent first offenses by someone in the boys' family or home were separately noted (see Table 21).

TABLE 21

LAPSE SINCE THE MOST RECENT FIRST OFFENSE BY ANYONE IN
THE IMMEDIATE FAMILY OR HOUSEHOLD

	Number	*Serious Offenses*
Under one year	73	47.9%
One year	38	65.8%
Two years	31	77.4%
Three years	22	54.5%
Four years and over	369	64.8%
No offenses by anyone	517	63.8%

None of these figures is significant, nor did correction for this aspect of the matter affect family percentages.

Special Detriments in Broken Homes

If a family is broken, new forces push themselves into the situation. How much time elapses before delinquent behavior begins? Does the boy acquire step-parents? Does his father help support the family, if he is still alive? How old was the boy when the home was broken?

ELAPSED TIME   After the break, what of the time element which represents the distance between breaking the family and breaking the law? This lapse may attenuate the effects of the breaks, and especially certain kinds. Further, the passage of time is filled with events; families are strengthened by recouping their organization or are weakened by repeated recognition of how much they have lost. When delinquency opportunities present themselves, they intersect these rising or falling curves of family social control at different points. These differences may be important.

Cases were divided between those broken under and over thirty-six months ago. There were sixty-eight cases with recent breaks, with a seriousness rate of 63.2 per cent. The rate for the others was 58.1 per cent; neither of these proportions is significant, nor did elapsed time affect any of the broken home subgroup percentages as a correction.

STEP-MOTHERS AND STEP-FATHERS   Folklore is rich in portrayals of step-parent wickedness. Real life also has its examples, as the case of one boy illustrates. He was a dull youngster of fifteen years, whose large, heavy step-mother had completely intimidated him. When the son was beaten and had his head shaven in punishment, his father stood by inertly, nor did he intervene when the boy was forced off to school with a sign on his neck saying, "I wet the bed." Not all step-parents are cruel; yet their presence produces new factors in family life. But these factors were found to have no significant relation to the boys' behavior, nor an effect upon the seriousness rates of family groups.[45] Nor did

The Results of Inequalities

it matter with which parent the boy was living, as the table following shows:

TABLE 22

STEP-PARENTS AT THE TIME OF DELINQUENCY

	Number	Serious Offenses
Boy with his mother	238	58.8%
No step-parent	126	59.5%
Step-Parent	75	56.0%
Paramour, etc.	37	62.2%
Boy with his father	68	60.3%
No step-parent	31	64.5%
Step-Parent	28	50.0%
Paramour, etc.	9	77.8%
Boy with foster parents	20	60.0%

Other aspects of the step-parent situation were reviewed. It was believed that support of the boy by the absent father might have meaning to the son, either in the connotation of the gesture of this support or in its economic impact. This might be reflected in the boy's behavior. Not all boys had equal access to help from their absent fathers; if the mother were married again the father might view his obligation to his son in a different way, or the support, if given, would have another meaning. There was, in fact, no relation to the boy's behavior (see Table 23).

WHEN HOME WAS BROKEN The following hypothesis was proposed by Whiting, Kluckhohn, and Anthony: "It has long been known that there is an association between certain types of juvenile delinquency and broken homes. We would predict that the probability of a boy becoming delinquent in such instances would be highest where the separation of the mother and father occurred during the early infancy of the boy and where she remarried when he was two or three years old."[46]

TABLE 23

ABSENT FATHER'S SUPPORT OF THE BOY

	Number	Serious Offenses
Father alive and step-father with boy		
Own father gave boy support	22	54.5%
Gave no support	50	56.0%
Father alive and no step-father with boy		
Own father gave boy support	38	55.3%
Gave no support	67	61.2%
Broken home, boy with father	68	60.3%
Father deceased	81	59.3%

Results reviewed in the immediately preceding section showed no relation between the presence of step-parents and delinquent behavior. What then of the age of the boy when his home was broken? Among cases, the relation of age at first break to delinquent behavior displayed this pattern:

Age at first break	Serious offenses—%	Age at first break	Serious offenses—%
Under 1	80.0	9	47.8
1	62.8	10	68.1
2	53.3	11	64.7
3	65.3	12	72.3
4	42.8	13	53.3
5	41.2	14	80.0
6	55.6	15	82.7
7	59.1	16	100.0
8	41.2		

There are three apparent groupings here: 0-3, 4-9 and 10-16. These and their distributions within family groupings are displayed in Table 24:

TABLE 24

Age at First Break in the Home

	0 - 3		4 - 9		10 - 16	
	Number	Serious Offenses	Number	Serious Offenses	Number	Serious Offenses
All broken	108	63.0%	127	48.8%	91	69.2%
Father dead	20	50.0%	27	59.3%	34	64.7%
Mother dead	14	71.4%	20	35.0%	19	63.2%
Parents divorced	31	58.1%	24	45.8%	10	70.0%
Parents separated	17	70.6%	33	45.5%	21	81.0%*
Father deserted	13	69.2%	14	42.9%	7	71.4%
Other condition	13	69.2%	9	77.8%	0	——

* This percentage is not significant.

None of the family per cents was changed in significant manner by correction in this array, nor were the seriousness rates for boys in the age-at-break groups 0-3 or 10-16 significantly high. However, ages 4-9 had a low rate which could not be ascribed to chance. This low rate was reflected in four of the family subgroups in the 4-9 column. Differences in distribution of cases by calendar period accounted for all of these low rates save for those where the mother died. Correction for time span changed the others to insignificant figures.

The low rate for maternal orphans was not explained by calendar period, nor the other factors of home supervision, neuroticism, disability of supervisors,[47] religious conflict of parents, birth of parents abroad, age at first delinquency, or boys' religious behavior. Boys whose mothers died when they were at this age were therefore a highly vulnerable group. To this degree the prediction made by Whiting, Kluckhohn, and Anthony receives support.

CHAPTER SEVEN

POTENTIALS FOR POLICY

The Significance of Divorce and Maternal Orphanhood

In all, 1,050 cases were studied, of which 326 were from broken homes. This is 31 per cent, which in itself precludes the broken home from being a general factor in delinquency. If the 139 unused cases—most of which were broken homes—are included, the percentage is 39 per cent. The broken home as such is important only in special aspects.

Correction by three of the variables lowered the rate for boys of divorce to a significant figure. The figure of 55.39 per cent was changed:

by boy's intelligence	to 50.72%	(p: 3.48%)
by type of supervision	to 50.08%	(p: 2.64%)
by calendar period of offense	to 50.91%	(p: 3.76%)

Early in this book, it was hypothesized that homes broken by divorce, separation, and desertion should have a greater proportion of minor offenders than others. It is wise not to base broad claims upon the results. The corrected percentages were just on the border; the lower confidence limit for the divorce group was 51.61 per cent, and all corrected percentages were just below this. It was not explained or explainable why these three controls affected divorce cases and not others. There was no consistent trend in the effect of other controls on this group. The controls had no significant effect upon similar breaks: separation and desertion. There was no religious connection here, for correction by religious affiliation produced no effect. Finally, the criterion percentage, 63.3, to which all comparisons were made was based in part on sampling, which reduces the impact of hairline differences. To sum up, the effect of these controls is consistent with one original hypothesis, but the evidence is not definitive.

It was also discovered that boys between the ages of four and nine whose homes were broken by death of the mother committed an especially low percentage of serious offenses. Yet eighteen cases only were involved, and this can be only a limited explanation of delinquent behavior, although meaningful for them.

Action on Delinquency

What of the boy who was described in the preface to this book? What can be done to help him? Has anything been learned to his benefit or to that of other boys as well? It was one purpose of this research to reveal the degree of importance to such a boy of his home being broken. The role of this break was found to be small, while certain other factors were of significant weight.

The relations of these factors to behavior and to each other are worthy of being analyzed in detail. A subsequent publication will do so. Now, this much can be said: Certain conditions were found to accompany minor offenses, and may be assumed to represent situations facilitating a high rate of delinquency. Others were associated with serious offenses, and are believed to include conditions in which delinquency is exceptional and low. These interpretations, which are still tentative, follow.

Differences in behavior by age reflect the interaction of maturation and social control. The low rate for those four to ten years of age expresses their immaturity; this group of delinquents probably represents inadequate supervision. Boys of this age can, for the most part, commit only offenses such as running away and general mischief; for them some petty larceny is possible, but they cannot commit serious acts prevalent among the older boys, such as sex offenses or taking a car without the owner's consent.

The high rate of serious offenses among those eleven to twelve years of age may represent the increased restraint placed upon youths as puberty nears, as well as the increase in age. The thirteen- to fifteen-year-old group is neither high nor low, and this may be explained as a reflection of the undermining of the prestige of adult authority by adolescent rebellion. The rate for the sixteen- to seventeen-year-old group is significantly high. In understanding this, we should recall that we are discussing first offenders. These are boys who were "good" for fifteen years, and then erupted into serious acts. Such a group of apparently well-behaved boys deserves special attention so that therapy may be applied to any who appear headed for delinquent behavior.

Boys with disabled and ill mothers appear to be a conforming group, if the data may be so interpreted; and when they become delinquent, they are likely to commit serious offenses. This is a group to be watched. Other things also were learned. Poor home supervision leads to delinquent behavior. Neurotic boys need control. Parental religious conflict reduces adherence to social norms. Lack of religious conviction is important among Protestant boys. Boys with both parents born abroad appear to be under stricter control. Only-boys from unbroken homes commit a very low proportion of serious offenses, available results indicate.

A Final Word

This study was based upon a group of white boys appearing in the Juvenile Court in an American city. They were examined in the light of their lives at the time of their first infraction of law. Evidence shows that a break in the home is not in general a crucial factor in the severity of a boy's misbehavior. Even when the home is broken, it is still able to control its children; perhaps other institutions in the community help in this. Delinquency cannot be fruitfully controlled through broad programs to prevent divorce or other breaks in family life. The prevention of these would certainly decrease unhappiness, but it would not help to relieve the problem of delinquency.

Appendices

APPENDIX A

Inferring Association through Comparison of Group Percentages

When groups are compared, one may speak of an association between the extent of delinquency, as represented in the sample, and the type of family situation. Shideler, for example, found that 50.8 per cent of the delinquents had broken homes compared with 25.3 per cent, estimated, of the general population of juveniles. It may be stated, "This study indicates that in this sample, there is a positive association between the extent of delinquency, and broken homes."

All of the authors cited in Chapter III, except Monahan, used a delinquent group and a non-delinquent comparison group. These may be considered two independent universes of observation. They may be compared by the test of the standard error of the difference between two proportions, the proportions being the percentages of given family situations:

$$\sqrt{\frac{\%_{p'} \times \%_{q'}}{N'} + \frac{\%_{p''} \times \%_{q''}}{N''}}$$

This same formula was applied to Monahan's data, which was from one universe, namely, cases before the court.

A different test, based on other assumptions and described in the text, was used in the present study.

APPENDIX B

Method of Assessing the Significances of Variations in the Incidences of Different Types of Broken Homes

The different types of breaks were tested for significances of the differences among their observed associations with delinquency, in the studies reviewed in Chapter III.

1. The percentage of each family situation among the delinquents and non-delinquents was determined. The studies used different classifications of breaks. These were taken as presented by the authors.
2. Types of breaks were ranked according to their relative prevalence among delinquents as compared to non-delinquents. See Table 1, for example.
3. The significances of the differences between types of breaks were determined. Each pair of breaks was taken as a sub-universe within the delinquent or non-delinquent universe. For example, in the material on which Table 1 is based, there were among the non-delinquents ten with both parents dead and 109 with father dead. Among these, those with both dead form 8.4 per cent of that total. For the delinquents, there were fifty-five with both parents dead and 294 with father dead. Of these, those with both parents dead form 15.8 per cent of that total.

   The difference in the percentages of both parents dead here was 7.4 per cent. The standard error of this difference is 3.3, so that the difference is significant at the 5 per cent level.
4. In Tables 1, 2 and 3, "*n*" means that such differences were not significant at the 5 per cent level. "*S*" means that they were significant at five per cent or less.

APPENDIX C

SERIOUS FIRST OFFENSES, BY FAMILY SITUATION; STATUS AT DELINQUENCY AND NATURE OF FIRST BREAK
(Includes only Broken Home Cases)

Status at Delinquency	Total –all Cases	First Break						
		Total Par. Died	Father Died	Mother Died	Total Div., etc.	Par. Div.	Par. Sep.	Father Deserted
ALL CASES								
Grand Total	326	132	81	51	194	38	102	54
% Serious	59.2	58.3	61.7	52.9	59.8	55.3	62.7	57.4
Total Parent Died	134	124	74	50	10	......	5	5
% Serious	57.5	57.3	60.8	52.0	60.0	......	100.0	20.0
Father Died	81	74	74	......	7	......	2	5
% Serious	59.3	60.8	60.8	......	42.9	......	100.0	20.0
Mother Died	53	50	......	50	3	......	3	......
% Serious	54.7	52.0	......	52.0	100.0	......	100.0	......
Total Divorce, etc.	170	......	......	......	170	29	95	46
% Serious	58.8	......	......	......	58.8	51.7	60.0	60.9
Divorce, etc.	65	......	......	......	65	29	25	11
% Serious	55.4	......	......	......	55.4	51.7	56.0	63.6
Separation	71	......	......	......	71	......	70	1
% Serious	62.0	......	......	......	62.0	......	61.4	100.0

Father Deserted	34	......	......	......	34	......	......	34
% Serious	58.8	......	......	......	58.8	......	......	58.8
Total Other	22	8	7	1	14	9	2	3
% Serious	72.7	75.0	71.4	100.0	71.4	66.7	100.0	66.7
Step-father Des.	20	7	7	......	13	9	1	3
% Serious	70.0	71.4	71.4	......	69.2	66.7	100.0	66.7
Step- or Foster Mother Died	2	1	......	1	1	......	1	......
% Serious	100.0	100.0	......	100.0	100.0	......	100.0	......
ONE BREAK								
Grand Total	252	124	74	50	128	29	66	33
% Serious	58.7	57.3	60.8	52.0	60.2	51.7	65.2	57.6
Total Parent Died	124	124	74	50	......	......	......	......
% Serious	57.3	57.3	60.8	52.0	......	......	......	......
Father Died	74	74	74	......	......	......	......	......
% Serious	60.8	60.8	60.8	......	......	......	......	......
Mother Died	50	50	......	50	......	......	......	......
% Serious	52.0	52.0	......	52.0	......	......	......	......
Total Divorce, etc.	128	......	......	......	128	29	66	33
% Serious	60.2	......	......	......	60.2	51.7	65.2	57.6
Divorce	29	......	......	......	29	29	......	......
% Serious	51.7	......	......	......	51.7	51.7	......	......

SERIOUS FIRST OFFENSES, BY FAMILY SITUATION; STATUS AT DELINQUENCY AND NATURE OF FIRST BREAK
(Includes only Broken Home Cases)—Continued

Status at Delinquency	First Break							
	Total –all Cases	Total Par. Died	Father Died	Mother Died	Total Div., etc.	Par. Div.	Par. Sep.	Father Deserted
Separation	66	......	......	......	66	......	66	......
% Serious	65.2	......	......	......	65.2	......	65.2	......
Father Deserted	33	......	......	......	33	......	......	33
% Serious	57.6	......	......	......	57.6	......	......	57.6
Total Other	......	......	......	......	......	......	......	......
% Serious	......	......	......	......	......	......	......	......
Step-father Des.	......	......	......	......	......	......	......	......
% Serious	......	......	......	......	......	......	......	......
Step- or Foster Mother Died	......	......	......	......	......	......	......	......
% Serious	......	......	......	......	......	......	......	......
TWO BREAKS								
Grand Total	74	8	7	1	66	9	36	21
% Serious	60.8	75.0	71.4	100.0	59.1	66.7	58.3	57.1
Total Parent Died	10	......	......	......	10	......	5	5
% Serious	60.0	......	......	......	60.0	......	100.0	20.0

Father Died	7		7			2	5
% Serious	42.9		42.9			100.0	20.0
Mother Died	3		3			3	3
% Serious	100.0		100.0			100.0	....
Total Divorce, etc.	42		42			29	13
% Serious	54.8		54.8			63.1	69.2
Divorce	36		36			25	11
% Serious	58.3		58.3			56.0	63.6
Separation	5		5			4	1
% Serious	20.0		20.0			0.0	100.0
Father Deserted	1		1	1			1
% Serious	100.0		100.0	100.0			100.0
Total Other	22	8	7	1	14	9	2	3
% Serious	72.7	75.0	71.4	100.0	71.4	66.7	100.0	66.7
Step-father Des.	20	7	7		13	9	1	3
% Serious	70.0	71.4	71.4		69.2	66.7	100.0	66.7
Step- or Foster Mother Died	2	1		1	1		1
% Serious	100.0	100.0		100.0	100.0		100.0

APPENDIX D

First Offenses Recorded among Cases, by Family Situation at Delinquency

Offenses	All Cases	Un-broken	Total Broken	Father Dead	Mother Dead	Par. Div.	Par. Sep.	Father Des.	Other Sit.
DISCIPLINE (Total)	371	244	127	31	23	28	27	13	5
Malicious Mischief	121	84	37	11	8	6	7	3	2
Truancy	37	16	21	6	5	2	4	3	1
Incorrigibility	49	32	17	6	3	1	6	1	...
False Alarm	39	36	3	...	...	...	3	...	...
Running Away	28	16	12	1	...	8	2	...	1
Disorderly Conduct	89	52	37	7	7	11	5	6	1
Trespassing	4	4	...	...	...	...	...	...	...
Indecent Language	4	4	...	...	...	...	...	...	...
ASSAULT	2	......	2	1	1	...	...	1	...
FORNICATION	12	8	4	1	1	1	...	...	1
LARCENY (Total)	344	256	88	20	16	16	16	13	7
Petty Larceny	186	144	42	8	10	5	9	9	1
Larceny	81	64	17	3	3	7	2	1	1
Grand Larceny	39	24	15	5	2	2	3	...	3
Selling Lottery Tickets	4	4	...	...	...	...	...	...	...

Offense									
Taking Auto without Consent of Owner	25	12	13	4	1	2	2	2	2
Receiving Stolen Goods	9	8	1	—	—	—	—	1	—
BURGLARY (Total)	242	164	78	20	10	14	21	5	8
Breaking, Entry, and Larceny	201	136	65	18	7	11	17	4	8
Entry and Larceny	29	20	9	2	1	1	4	1	—
Breaking and Entry	12	8	4	—	2	2	—	—	—
SERIOUS SEX OFFENSES (Total)	58	40	18	6	2	5	4	—	1
Carnal Abuse	10	4	6	3	—	2	1	—	—
Fellatio	43	32	11	3	2	3	2	—	1
Indecent Exposure	5	4	1	—	—	—	1	—	—
CARRYING CONCEALED WEAPONS	1	—	1	—	—	1	—	—	—
ATROCIOUS ASSAULT AND BATTERY	8	4	4	1	—	—	2	1	—
ARSON	9	8	1	—	—	—	1	—	—
ROBBERY	3	—	3	1	1	—	—	1	—
TOTAL	1050	724	326	81	53	65	71	34	22

APPENDIX E

Correcting for Differences between Subgroups and the Study Universe in the Distribution of Control Variables

Correction for a variable is effected by weighting the cells in subgroups according to the distribution of the control variable in the whole. Its mathematical expression is shown in the formula below. It is said in effect, "If all groups had equal composition, according to this control factor, what would be their serious offense percentages?"

A corrected per cent is:

$$\left[\sum \frac{A_1 B_1 C_1}{A_1 C_1} \times \frac{C_1}{N} \times \frac{100}{\Sigma(A_1 C_1/A)} \right]$$

where: $A_1 B_1 C_1$ is the number of cases with serious offenses in any given family subgroup exhibiting the given aspect of the control factor (or other subdivision, as specified)

$A_1 C_1$ is the total number of cases in the same cell

C_1 is the total number of cases in N exhibiting the given aspect of the control factor

N is all cases in the study (1,050, or other number in subsidiary analyses)

A is the total number of cases in any given family subgroup.

Appendix E

The formula is based in the main on G. Udny Yule and Maurice G. Kendall, *Introduction to the Theory of Statistics* (14th edition, revised; New York: Hafner Publishing Company, 1950), pp. 335-37.

The first factor corrects the percentages of serious offenses in family groups, supposing the control distribution of all to be equal. The second factor compensates for vacant cells. For example, there was no boy aged four to seven with a dead mother in the array for correction for age. Without compensation, the weighted percentage would have been deficient on this account; the factor expanded the sum of the other age products to a proportion of 100 per cent. Where no cells are empty, this factor is unity. Alternate techniques were used in some instances, as explained in those cases. Correction was not always applied to family subgroups where the probable results did not promise to warrant the IBM or calculational work involved.

Characteristics of the sample of unbroken homes were weighted by four to give them their proper proportion, as explained in Chapter V. Tests of significance were the same as described in that place, and were based on N_s defined as the actual and not the expanded number of cases.

APPENDIX F

CORRECTED PERCENTAGES PRODUCED BY CONTROL FACTORS*

Factor	Un-broken	Total Broken	Father Dead	Mother Dead	Parents Div.	Parents Sep.	Father Des.	Other Sit.
Age at First Break in the Home			57.7	54.9	56.6	63.7	59.6	73.9
Age at First Known Offense	63.8	58.4	58.7	53.8	54.8	64.0	64.5	76.7
Calendar Period in which Act Committed	64.8	59.8	59.7	54.7	50.9	66.2	58.4	76.1
Change in Juvenile Court Age, July, 1948	65.0	59.5						
Companions in the Act	64.6	60.0						
Delinquency Rates by Residence Wards	64.0	59.3	59.2	55.3	56.7	64.4	59.1	72.0
Disabilities of Father Figures with Boys	65.1	57.9						
Disabilities of Mother Figures with Boys	64.6	59.2						
Disabilities of Non-Family Household Members	65.3	58.1						
Disabilities of Siblings	65.2	59.2						
Disabilities of Supervisors	64.7	59.4						

	1	2	3	4	5	6	7	8
Elapsed Time between Break and Delinquency								
Employment of Boy	65.3	58.8	59.5	55.8	54.5	60.4	58.8	73.7
Foreign-Born Parents	65.2	61.1	59.9	54.1	54.6	61.8	58.3	74.9
Head of Household—Identity of	66.6	60.6	57.1	56.1	52.2	66.8	55.3	76.8
Intelligence of Boy	65.5	60.0	59.1	57.4	50.7	62.1	60.3	75.8
Mental Problems of Boy	65.5	58.7	59.4	53.9	55.0	61.9	56.7	69.8
Moves of Boy's Household	65.5	59.5	59.6	54.3	52.9	66.0	63.6	71.5
Number of Siblings	64.2	58.5						
Occupation of Chief Wage Earner	67.2	58.7	57.0	55.8	56.3	63.3	61.9	78.0
Offenses—Anyone in the Family or Household	65.3	59.6	59.3	52.3	56.8	65.7	53.0	77.5
Offenses—of Father	65.1	59.8	58.6	52.6	58.0	65.0	53.3	73.7
Offenses—Lapse since a First by Anyone in Family or Household	65.6	59.2						
Offenses—of Mother	63.1	59.5						
Offenses—of Siblings	64.5	58.8						
Ordinal Position among Siblings	64.1	59.6	58.8	57.6	51.9	60.7	61.2	74.0

Corrected Percentages Produced by Control Factors*—Continued

Factor	Un-broken	Total Broken	Father Dead	Mother Dead	Parents Div.	Parents Sep.	Father Des.	Other Sit.
Physical Problems of Boy	65.7	59.4						
Relative Position among Siblings	64.0	59.1						
Relief and Aid to the Family	66.5	58.3	56.9	51.7	59.7	57.8	60.5	69.0
Religious Affiliation and Interest of Boy	65.5	59.5	59.5	54.1	58.0	62.9	60.8	70.4
Religious Conflict of Parents	65.0	63.8						
Step-Parents, and with Whom at Delinquency			57.5	53.5	58.5	65.1	63.8	70.7
Step-Siblings in the Home	64.5	59.4	59.0	57.0	58.6	61.0	60.0	79.4
Supervision	64.9	60.2	61.1	59.7	50.1	58.3	59.7	71.0
Unofficial and Adult Court Cases	65.2	59.1	60.1	55.4	55.4	61.3	58.1	72.7

* Corrected percentages are shown where they were computed; figures were not prepared where distributions were extremely scattered or where inconsequential results were to be expected in the basis of other distributions.

The corrected percentages which are shown in the table are based on detailed tabulations; these are available in the author's doctoral dissertation, "Broken Homes and the Violation of Delinquency Norms in First Offenses among Juveniles" (University of Pennsylvania, 1962).

Notes

NOTES

NOTES FOR CHAPTER ONE

1. Richard B. Morris, *Encyclopedia of American History* (New York: Harper and Brothers, 1953), p. 544.

2. W. D. Morrison, *Juvenile Offenders* (London: T. Fisher Unwin, 1896), pp. 146-47.

3. Sophonisba P. Breckinridge and Edith Abbott, *The Delinquent Child and the Home* (New York: Russell Sage Foundation, 1912), p. 90-91.

4. William Healy, *The Individual Delinquent* (Boston: Little, Brown and Company, 1915), pp. 290-91.

5. William Healy and Augusta Bronner, *Delinquents and Criminals: Their Making and Unmaking* (New York: The Macmillan Company, 1926), p. 123.

6. Ernest H. Shideler, "Family Disintegration and the Delinquent Boy in the United States," *Journal of Criminal Law and Criminology*, VIII (January, 1918), 709-32.

7. George B. Mangold, *Problems of Child Welfare* (rev. ed.; New York: The Macmillan Company, 1924), p. 406.

8. Clifford R. Shaw and Henry D. McKay, "Social Factors in Juvenile Delinquency," National Commission on Law Observance and Enforcement, *Report on the Causes of Crime*, No. 13, II (Washington, 1931).

9. *Ibid.*, 276.

10. H. Ashley Weeks and Margaret G. Smith, "Juvenile Delinquency and Broken Homes in Spokane, Washington," *Social Forces*, XVIII (October, 1939), 48-55. See p. 48.

11. Negley K. Teeters and John Otto Reinemann, *The Challenge of Delinquency* (New York: Prentice-Hall, Inc., 1950), p. 154.

12. Carl M. Rosenquist, *Social Problems* (New York: Prentice-Hall, Inc., 1940), p. 454.

13. Sheldon Glueck and Eleanor T. Glueck, *Unraveling Juvenile Delinquency* (New York: The Commonwealth Fund, 1950), p. 123.

14. G. Lewis Penner, "An Experiment in Police and Social Agency Cooperation," *The Annals of the American Academy of Political and Social Science*, CCCXXII (March, 1959), 79-88. See p. 85.

15. Essex County Juvenile and Domestic Relations Court, *Problems Presented in the Juvenile and Domestic Relations Court. Annual Report, 1955* (Newark, N. J., 1955), p. 19.

16. Children's Bureau, Department of Health, Education and Welfare, *Report to Congress on Juvenile Delinquency* (Washington, D. C.: U. S. G. P. O., 1960), p. 21.

17. *Ibid.*, p. 5.

18. *Ibid.*, p. 7.

NOTES FOR CHAPTER TWO

1. Thorsten Sellin, *Culture Conflict and Crime,* Social Science Research Council, Bulletin No. 41 (New York, 1938), Chap. IV. The concept is extended here to include "compulsion potentials" as well as "resistance potentials."

2. An interesting approach to this problem which aims to extend the area of detected offenses has been developed by several authors. See F. Ivan Nye, "Child Adjustment in Broken and in Unhappy Unbroken Homes," *Marriage and Family Living,* XIX (November, 1957), 356-61; *Family Relationships and Delinquent Behavior* (New York: John Wiley and Sons, 1958); and Robert A. Dentler and Lawrence J. Monroe, "Early Adolescent Theft," *American Sociological Review,* XXVI (October, 1961), 733-43. These contain studies based upon the self-reports of school children on their delinquencies. The authors have not validated the accuracy of these confessions, wherefore the results are inconclusive. See also, Jackson Toby, review of F. Ivan Nye's book in the *American Sociological Review,* XXIV (April, 1959), 282-83.

3. Paul W. Tappan, *Juvenile Delinquency* (New York: The McGraw-Hill Book Company, 1949), p. 5.

4. The administration of juvenile correction complicates the picture. Sentences are not passed, and the juvenile is not termed guilty of such and such an offense. But the judge's conclusions are based mainly on the norms. He says in effect, "This act is highly prohibited by teaching and by law. A boy who does that must truly need correctional treatment." Of another it is said, "This act is lightly prohibited. Many children could be as antisocial as that." There are exceptions, based on individual investigations; but, whatever happens, the usual juvenile sees court action as punishment, and expects there to be a proportion between his act and the result.

5. William C. Kvaraceus and Walter B. Miller, *Delinquent Behavior: Culture and the Individual,* National Education Association of the United States (Washington, D. C., 1959), p. 65.

It may also be objected that one particular delinquency or another is not attractive to a given juvenile, and the scale of resistance potentials, as expressed in teaching and law, does not relate in full to his attitudes. Yet most offenders know which possible individual choices are more highly forbidden than others, and they have the same relative positions as in the complete scale.

6. Milton L. Barron, "Juvenile Delinquency and American Values," *American Sociological Review,* XVI (April, 1951), 208-14. See also Eleanor E. Maccoby, Joseph P. Johnson, and Russell M. Church, "Community Integration and the Social Control of Juvenile Delinquency," *Journal of Social Issues,* XIV, No. 3 (1958), 38-51. See p. 49.

7. Walter C. Reckless, "A Non Causal Explanation: Containment Theory," *Excerpta Criminologica,* II (March-April, 1962), 131-34. Albert J. Reiss, Jr., "Delinquency as the Failure of Personal and Social Controls," *American Sociological Review,* XVI (April, 1951), 196-207.

8. Richard S. Sterne, *Outcome of Parole as Related to Pre-Parole Prognosis* (Philadelphia: Pennsylvania Committee on Penal Affairs, 1946). See pp. 10 and 11.

9. Sheldon Glueck and Eleanor T. Glueck, *Unraveling Juvenile Delinquency* (New York: The Commonwealth Fund, 1950), p. 131; Table XI-22. See comments on the Gluecks' book in Chapter III.

10. David J. Bordua, *Sociological Theories and Their Implications for Juvenile Delinquency,* U. S. Department of Health, Education and Welfare, (Washington, D. C., 1960), p. 4. See also Richard A. Cloward and Lloyd E. Ohlin, *Delinquency and Opportunity* (Glencoe, Ill.: The Free Press, 1960). See in particular, pp. 139-43.

11. Orville S. Walters, "The Religious Background of Fifty Alcoholics," *Quarterly Journal of Studies on Alcohol,* XVIII (September, 1957), 405-16.

12. Selden D. Bacon, "Social Settings Conducive to Alcoholism," *Journal of the American Medical Association,* CLXIV (May 11, 1957), 177-81.

13. Harold T. Christensen, "Cultural Relativism and Premarital Sex Norms," *American Sociological Review,* XXV (February, 1960), 31-39.

14. Mabel A. Elliott, *Correctional Education and the Delinquent Girl*, Pennsylvania Department of Welfare, Bulletin No. 36 (Harrisburg, Pennsylvania, 1929).

15. Albert K. Cohen, *Delinquent Boys* (Glencoe, Ill.: The Free Press, 1955), pp. 163-65.

16. McCord and Zola discuss the relation of home discipline to the incidence and type of crime. However, their cases are not numerous. Also, it is not possible to translate their categories of offenses and discipline into those given here. For example, they use the group "property offenses." Some such offenses, e.g., malicious mischief, are not serious. See William McCord and Joan McCord, with Irving Kenneth Zola, *Origins of Crime* (New York: Columbia University Press, 1959), p. 155, Table 77.

17. Donald R. Taft, *Criminology* (New York: The Macmillan Company, 1950), pp. 143-44.

18. See Reuben Hill, *Families Under Stress* (New York: Harper and Brothers, 1949), pp. 232-33. See also F. Ivan Nye, *op. cit.* (1957).

NOTES FOR CHAPTER THREE

1. Ernest Shideler, "Family Disintegration and the Delinquent Boy in the United States," *Journal of Criminal Law and Criminology*, VIII (January, 1918), 709-32. Reviews in this chapter include statistical tests of significance of the findings reported. These were not applied to Shideler's material, in which comparisons were based on census estimates, not definite data.

2. *Ibid.*

3. John Slawson, *The Delinquent Boy* (Boston: Richard G. Badger, Publisher, 1926).

4. *Ibid.*, p. 369.

5. *Ibid.*, Table 64, p. 354; and Table 64B, p. 366.

6. See Appendices A and B for description of statistical methods used in this chapter.

7. Mabel A. Elliott and Francis E. Merrill, *Social Disorganization* (3rd ed.; New York: Harper and Brothers, 1950), p. 76.

8. Mabel A. Elliott, *Correctional Education and the Delinquent Girl*, Pennsylvania Department of Welfare, Bulletin No. 36 (Harrisburg, Pa., 1929).

9. Hazel Grant Ormsbee, *The Young Employed Girl* (New York: The Womans Press, 1927).

10. Clifford R. Shaw and Henry D. McKay, "Social Factors in Juvenile Delinquency," National Commission on Law Observance and Enforcement, *Report on the Causes of Crime*, No. 13, II (Washington: 1931), 261-63.

11. William S. Robinson, "Ecological Correlations and the Behavior of Individuals," *American Sociological Review*, XV (June, 1950), 351-57; Leo A. Goodman, "Ecological Regressions and Behavior of Individuals," *American Sociological Review*, XVIII (December, 1953), 663-64.

12. *Op. cit.*, pp. 275-76.

13. Julius B. Maller, "Are Broken Homes a Causative Factor in Juvenile Delinquency? IV. Discussion," *Social Forces*, X (May, 1932), 531-33.

14. Jackson Toby, "The Differential Impact of Family Disorganization," *American Sociological Review*, XXII (October, 1957), 505-12.

15. Joanna C. Colcord, "Are Broken Homes a Causative Factor in Juvenile Delinquency? I. Discussion," *Social Forces*, X (May, 1932), 525-27.

16. Harry M. Shulman, "Are Broken Homes a Causative Factor in Juvenile Delinquency? III. Discussion," *Social Forces*, X (May, 1932), 529-30.

17. *Op. cit.*

18. *Op. cit.*, p. 273.

19. *Ibid.*, p. 279, Table XXXIX.

20. Margaret Hodgkiss, "The Influence of Broken Homes and Working Mothers," *Smith College Studies in Social Work*, III (March, 1933), 259-74.

21. H. Ashley Weeks and Margaret G. Smith, "Juvenile Delinquency and Broken Homes in Spokane, Washington," *Social Forces*, XVIII (October, 1939), 48-55.

22. 4th ed.; London: University of London Press, Ltd., 1944. See table; p. 64 in Burt's book.

23. Yonkers-on-Hudson: World Book Company, 1945.

24. Sheldon Glueck and Eleanor T. Glueck, *Unraveling Juvenile Delinquency* (New York: The Commonwealth Fund, 1950), p. 133.

25. *Ibid.*, p. 78.

26. *Ibid.*, p. 35.

27. *Ibid.*, p. 80.

28. *Ibid.*, p. 103.

29. *Ibid.*, p. 104.

30. *Ibid.*, p. 106.

31. *Ibid.*, p. 81.

32. *Ibid.*, p. 36.

33. *Ibid.*, p. 36.

34. Albert J. Reiss, Jr., "Unraveling Juvenile Delinquency–An Appraisal of the Research Methods," *American Journal of Sociology,* LVII (September, 1951), 115-20. Also see Sol Rubin, "Unraveling Juvenile Delinquency–Illusions in a Research Project," *American Journal of Sociology,* LVII (September, 1951), 107-14.

35. The Gluecks provide this material on page 123, *op. cit.* Tabulations on pages 91 and 124, *Ibid.*, show current parental marital statuses and the nature of all breaches in family life. The material examined in this review is closer in content to other studies reviewed.

36. Thomas P. Monahan, "Family Status and the Delinquent Child: A Reappraisal and Some New Findings," *Social Forces,* XXXV (March, 1957), 250-58.

37. Sophonisba P. Breckinridge and Edith Abbott, *The Delinquent Child and the Home* (New York: Russell Sage Foundation, 1912). Material given here is based upon the Appendix to the report entitled "Family Paragraphs Relating to the Delinquency of 100 Boys," pp. 267-313.

38. Russell Sage Foundation, *Boyhood and Lawlessness* (New York, 1914), Appendix.

39. H. Ashley Weeks, "Male and Female Broken Home Rates by Type of Delinquency," *American Sociological Review,* V (August, 1940), 601-9. The distribution of girls' offenses did not allow for analysis in this review. See additional discussion in Chapter VI, footnote 4.

40. *Op. cit.*, p. 373, Table 65.

41. *Ibid.*, p. 374, Table 66.

42. *Op. cit.*, Table 3.

43. *Op. cit.*

NOTES FOR CHAPTER FOUR

1. William W. Wattenburg, "Juvenile Repeaters from Two Viewpoints," *American Sociological Review,* XVIII (December, 1953), 631-35.

2. In the pilot study of thirty-five cases, the worst offenders were from badly disorganized homes. This included the illegitimate, the homeless, and the frequently shifted to new foster

parents. These were the worst by any measure—offense, recidivism, and judgments of psychiatrists and case workers. Next came children with both parents together, then those of divorce, and last, those with one or both parents dead. In this small sample, no differences were produced by control of sex, age, religion, color, or income of parents.

3. Bureau of Juvenile Aid, Trenton, N.J. Department of Police, *Annual Report* (Trenton, N.J., 1957).

The word "serious" used in reference to the data in this paragraph is defined in the next chapter.

4. Mercer County Probation Office, *Annual Report, 1957*, (Trenton, N.J., 1958).

5. Reuben Hill, *Families Under Stress* (New York: Harper and Brothers, 1949), pp. 61-64.

6. Questions have been raised by Philip M. Smith ("Broken Homes and Delinquency," *Sociology and Social Research,* XXXIX [May, 1955], 307-11) regarding bias in delinquency studies caused by differential treatment of children according to family situation. This is discussed in Chapter VI of this book.

NOTES FOR CHAPTER FIVE

1. Sheldon Glueck and Eleanor T. Glueck, *Unraveling Juvenile Delinquency* (New York: The Commonwealth Fund, 1950), pp. 28, 293.

2. John Slawson, *The Delinquent Boy* (Boston: Richard G. Badger, Publisher, 1926), pp. 169-72.

3. Willis W. Clark, *The Whittier Scale for Grading Juvenile Offenses,* Whittier State School Bureau of Juvenile Research, Bulletin No. 11, April, 1922. [Cited in abstract in the *Journal of Delinquency,* VII (November, 1922), 364.]

4. Melvin A. Durea, "An Experimental Study of Attitudes Toward Juvenile Delinquency," *Journal of Applied Psychology,* XVII (October, 1933), 522-34.

5. Edwin Powers and Helen L. Witmer, *An Experiment in the Prevention of Delinquency—The Cambridge-Somerville Youth Study* (New York: Columbia University Press, 1951), pp. 328-32.

6. Melvin A. Durea, "A Quantitative Method of Diagnosing the Seriousness of Asocial Behavior of Juvenile Delinquents," *Journal of General Psychology,* XIV (April, 1936), 412-20.

7. There are pitfalls in more complex operations. Powers and Witmer, *loc. cit.*, rate trespassing 1.13 and manslaughter 4.00. Scores were averaged and combined. This is not valid, because 3.54 trespasses do not equal one manslaughter.

8. Appreciation is expressed to Dr. Edwin P. Hutchinson for suggestions in formulating the procedure used here. The "layer" method was also tried with results substantially similar to those reported on the following pages. See Thomas A. Ryan, "Significance Tests for Multiple Comparison of Proportions, Variances, and Other Statistics," *Psychological Bulletin*, LVII (July, 1960), 318-28.

NOTES FOR CHAPTER SIX

1. The corrected percentage for this control factor for the divorce group is shown later as 50.1 per cent. The difference is caused by grouping of supervisional situations in the short table given here.

2. Technical details of procedures employed are presented in Appendix E, to which the reader may refer.

Control variables themselves were compared to behavior, by the tests on pp. 58-9. Thus, in Table 4, no divorce cell was significant, but for all boys, poor supervision was, as stated in the text.

3. Essex County Juvenile and Domestic Relations Court, *Problems Presented in the Juvenile and Domestic Relations Court. Annual Report, 1955* (Newark, N. J., 1955).

4. The weight of this point has been lessened by Weeks, though his evidence is not conclusive. See H. Ashley Weeks, "Male and Female Broken Home Rates by Type of Delinquency," *American Sociological Review*, V (August, 1940), 601-9. His female subjects' offenses included (*a*) ungovernable, running away, and truancy, and (*b*) other offenses. Offenses of males included (*a*) ungovernable, running away, and truancy, (*b*) traffic, (*c*) misdemeanors, and (*d*) others. The number of cases permitted no closer comparisons. The broken home rates for (*a*) boys and (*a*) girls were closer than for boys and girls at large, but girls were still higher. Weeks suggests this was caused by differential police and correctional action. There is, if so, an effect if not a cause, which requires experimental control.

5. Mercer County Probation Office, *Annual Report, 1957* (Trenton, N. J., 1958).

Notes

6. *Ibid.*

7. Thorsten Sellin, "Race Prejudice in the Administration of Justice," *American Journal of Sociology*, XLI (September, 1935), 212-17.

8. Elsa Castendyck and Sophia M. Robison, "Juvenile Delinquency Among Girls," *Social Service Review*, XVII (September, 1943), 253-64.

9. E. Franklin Frazier, *The Negro Family in the United States* (Chicago: University of Chicago Press, 1939).

10. Harold A. Phelps, *Contemporary Social Problems* (New York: Prentice-Hall, Inc., 1946), pp. 573-74, 625.

11. William McCord and Joan McCord, with Irving Kenneth Zola, *Origins of Crime* (New York: Columbia University Press, 1959), p. 167.

12. Some studies have ranked subjects by school achievement or retardation. This may involve error. Goodlad shows that dull children may be promoted or not by the school (See John Inkster Goodlad, "Research and Theory Regarding Promotion and Non-Promotion," *Elementary School Journal*, LIII [November, 1952], 150-55). Administrative and policy decisions affect the assignment of children. Further, in Trenton there are ungraded classes for the dull, which preclude specific ratings of retardation in terms of school grades.

13. Corrected percentages for family groupings are given in Appendix F for this control factor and for all others.

14. A special tabulation was made of cases divided by the time periods 1937-48 and 1949-59, and by the age groups four to fifteen and sixteen to seventeen. It was found that sixteen to seventeen-year-olds were in smaller proportion in the earlier period. However, they committed a relatively greater percentage of serious offenses in both time periods. The rates for unbroken and total broken homes were not affected by correction according to this distribution.

15. Edwin H. Sutherland and Donald R. Cressey, *Principles of Criminology* (Philadelphia: J. B. Lippincott Company, 1955), p. 192.

16. Sophia M. Robison, *Can Delinquency Be Measured?* (New York: Columbia University Press, 1936), p. 32.

17. Joseph A. Kahl and James A. Davis, "A Comparison of Indexes of Socio-Economic Status," *American Sociological Review*, XX (June, 1955), 317-25.

18. U. S. Bureau of the Census, *1950 Census of Population:*

Classified Index of Occupations and Industries (Washington, D. C., 1950).

19. The head of the household usually was the father, the step-father, the mother or foster mother. Sometimes it was the widowed mother's brother or some other relation. In 759 families where father was head, the seriousness rate was 64.4 per cent; step-father, 71, 54.9 per cent; mother, 177, 59.3 per cent; other persons 43, 74.4 per cent. None of these figures is significant.

20. John A. Clausen and Marion R. Yarrow, eds., "Impact of Mental Illness in the Family (Symposium)," *Journal of Social Issues*, XI, No. 4 (1955), 3-64.

21. All mother figures were combined in this tabulation; there were no appreciable differences between seriousness rates for mothers, step-mothers, foster mothers, or other such figures for these data.

22. The relation of the boys' own physical illnesses and mental difficulties to those of their families was probed. One hundred and thirteen boys had some known somatic complaint or history or illness. In all, their seriousness rate was 63.6 per cent. There was some indication that the more serious illnesses were associated with the more serious offenses, but the number of cases was too small to support this conclusion.

Table 11 shows that the seriousness rate for boys with mentally abnormal mothers was low, though not significantly so; the same trend was discovered with other family and household members. One hundred and four boys, for example, had supervisors showing mental disturbances, and had a rate of 56.7 per cent. One hundred and three boys were neurotic themselves, with a rate of 31.1 per cent. These two groups overlapped in fifteen cases, and among this duplicate group the rate was 46.7 per cent. The boys' neuroses and related behavior did not appear to be aspects of the overt disturbances of others at home.

23. No relation to behavior was found in birthplace of parent figures where one was a step- or a foster parent. Therefore, all of these cases were grouped in Table 13. It would have been desirable to have related behavior to the ethnic extractions of the boys themselves. Too few were themselves foreign-born to analyze this, and individual ethnic affiliations were not regularly specified in the records. Also, if a boy were described as "Italian," for instance, he might or might not have identified himself with that group.

24. Sophia M. Robison, "The Apparent Effects of the Factors of Race and Nationality on the Registration of Behavior as Delinquent in New York City in 1930," *Publication of the American Sociological Society*, XXVIII (May, 1934), 37-44.

25. It was explained in an earlier chapter that the rate for the 139 unused homes had a non-significant rate of 61.3 per cent, based on a 25 per cent sample. There also were no trends in control variable relations inconsistent with those reported here.

26. Harry Elmer Barnes, *Social Institutions* (Philadelphia: Prentice-Hall, Inc., 1942), p. 647.

27. Use of areas smaller than wards would have been desirable. Data were not available for such a procedure, since police statistics on arrests were kept only by wards. In Trenton there are fourteen wards and twenty-four residential Census Tracts; the boundaries of these do not coincide in any manner permitting transposition of data from the first to the second system.

28. U. S. Bureau of the Census, *U. S. Census of Population, 1930*, Vol. III, *Characteristics of the Population*, Part 2, *Report by States* (Washington, D. C., 1932), p. 224.

29. U. S. Bureau of the Census, *U. S. Census of Population, 1940*, Vol. II, *Characteristics of the Population*, Part 4, *Report by States* (Washington, D. C., 1942), pp. 902, 904.

30. U. S. Bureau of the Census, unpublished tabulation of population by age and by ward, for the City of Trenton, New Jersey, for 1950.

31. The age spans for juvenile arrests were not the same for all years, because of the change in Juvenile Court age in 1948. This caused no bias in the results reported herein, since ward-year rates were compared only to the totals for the same years. If a ward rate went up because of the change, so did the total rate. Comparisons of wards to themselves from year to year were not made for an additional reason. Great changes occurred in areas. For example, Ward 7 in 1937 included a group of stable mid-city homes. Social changes had turned it into a business district by 1950, where the only homes were blighted boarding rooms and flats. In the earlier year the Ward 7 rate for arrests was average; by 1943 it rose above average, where it stayed. Ward 3 shifted from a Jewish to a mixed area; Ward 6 changed from Jewish to Polish; Wards 8 and 9 had several troublesome families in certain years, which affected their rates.

32. Ernest R. Mowrer, *Disorganization: Personal and Social* (Philadelphia: J. B. Lippincott Company, 1942), pp. 207-12.

33. Sophia M. Robison, *Can Delinquency Be Measured?* (New York: Columbia University Press, 1936), p. 228.

34. Clifford R. Shaw and Henry D. McKay, "Social Factors in Juvenile Delinquency," National Commission on Law Observance and Enforcement, *Report on the Causes of Crime*, No. 13, II (Washington, D. C., 1931), 195-96.

35. Sheldon and Eleanor T. Glueck, *Unraveling Juvenile Delinquency* (New York: The Commonwealth Fund, 1950), p. 164.

36. Katherine F. Lenroot, "Are Broken Homes a Causative Factor in Juvenile Delinquency? II. Discussion," *Social Forces*, X (May, 1932), 527-29.

37. Harry Elmer Barnes and Negley K. Teeters, *New Horizons in Criminology* (New York: Prentice-Hall, Inc., 1945), p. 213.

38. Alvin L. Schorr, "Mobile Family Living," *Social Casework*, XXXVII (April, 1956), 175-80.

39. Martha Bushfield VanValen, "An Approach to Mobile Dependent Families," *Social Casework*, XXXVII (April, 1956), 180-86.

40. T. J. Woofter, Jr., "Size of Family in Relation to Family Income and Age of Family Head," *American Sociological Review*, IX (December, 1944), 678-84. See Table 6.

41. William W. Wattenburg, "Delinquency and Only Children, a Study of a 'Category'," *Journal of Abnormal and Social Psychology*, XLIV (July, 1949), 356-66.

42. *Op. cit.*, p. 118.

43. William Healy and Augusta Bronner, *Delinquents and Criminals: Their Making and Unmaking* (New York: The Macmillan Company, 1926), p. 104. The reason for difference by family size was not specified. The authors' earlier work, on which these figures were based, was consulted, but this did not provide clarification. See "A Comparative Study of Two Groups, Each of 1000 Young Recidivists," *American Journal of Sociology*, XX (July, 1916), 38-52.

44. *Op. cit.*, pp. 101-2.

45. Step-parents include those in common-law marriage with the remaining parent. "Common-law marriages" were those in which the partners represented themselves as married, and as a family, sharing bed, board, and income. Few of the new unions in the divorced, father dead, or mother dead were of this kind; most of those in the separated, father deserted, and "other" situations were. However, there was no association between the legality of the union and the step-son's behavior. Orphans and boys of divorce had fifty step-fathers and twenty-seven step-mothers. Boys

in these groups had rates of 54.0 per cent and 48.2 per cent re-spectively. Among the boys with homes broken by desertion, separation or other cause, twenty-five had step-fathers, and had a rate of 60.0 per cent; one had a step-mother, and had com-mitted a serious act. None of these percentages is significant.

Paramours, shown in Table 22, included irregular relationships and other contacts of this sort. Foster parents included relatives or others than a real parent (or step-parent), with whom the boy went to live.

The possibility of common-law marriages of the boys' natural parents was examined for use as a control factor. However, such situations were found in only thirteen of the 1,050 cases and no further consideration was given to the matter.

46. John W. M. Whiting, Richard Kluckhohn, and Albert An-thony, "The Function of Male Initiation Ceremonies at Puberty," *Readings in Social Psychology* (New York: Holt, Rinehart and Winston, Inc., 1958; Eleanor E. Maccoby, Theodore M. New-comb, and Eugene L. Hartley, eds.), pp. 359-70. See p. 370.

47. Few of the maternal orphans had mother figures in the home. Disability of supervisors was used here as a test.

SELECTED REFERENCES

SELDEN D. BACON. "Social Settings Conducive to Alcoholism," *Journal of the American Medical Association,* CLXIV (May 11, 1957), 177-81.

HARRY ELMER BARNES. *Social Institutions* (Philadelphia: Prentice-Hall, Inc., 1942).

———— and NEGLEY K. TEETERS. *New Horizons in Criminology* (New York: Prentice-Hall, Inc., 1945).

MILTON L. BARRON. "Juvenile Delinquency and American Values," *American Sociological Review,* XVI (April, 1951), 208-14.

DAVID J. BORDUA. *Sociological Theories and Their Implications for Juvenile Delinquency,* U.S. Department of Health, Education and Welfare, Washington, D.C., 1960).

SOPHONISBA P. BRECKINRIDGE and EDITH ABBOTT. *The Delinquent Child and the Home* (New York: Russell Sage Foundation, 1912).

Bureau of Juvenile Aid, Trenton, N.J. Department of Police, *Annual Report* (Trenton, N.J., 1957).

CYRIL BURT. *The Young Delinquent* (4th ed.; London: University of London Press, Ltd., 1944).

ELSA CASTENDYCK and SOPHIA M. ROBISON. "Juvenile Delinquency Among Girls," *Social Service Review,* XVII (September, 1943), 253-64.

Children's Bureau, Department of Health, Education and Welfare, *Report to Congress on Juvenile Delinquency* (Washington, D.C.: U.S.G.P.O., 1960).

HAROLD T. CHRISTENSEN. "Cultural Relativism and Premarital Sex Norms," *American Sociological Review,* XXV (February, 1960), 31-39.

WILLIS W. CLARK. *The Whittier Scale for Grading Juvenile Offenses,* Whittier State School Bureau of Juvenile Research, Bulletin No. 11, April, 1922. (Cited in abstract in the *Journal of Delinquency*, VII [November, 1922], 364.)

JOHN A. CLAUSEN and MARION R. YARROW, eds. "Impact of Mental Illness in the Family" (Symposium), *Journal of Social Issues*, XI, No. 4 (1955), 3-64.

RICHARD A. CLOWARD and LLOYD E. OHLIN. *Delinquency and Opportunity* (Glencoe, Ill.: The Free Press, 1960).

ALBERT K. COHEN. *Delinquent Boys* (Glencoe, Ill.: The Free Press, 1955).

JOANNA C. COLCORD. "Are Broken Homes a Causative Factor in Juvenile Delinquency? I. Discussion," *Social Forces*, X (May, 1932), 525-27.

ROBERT A. DENTLER and LAWRENCE J. MONROE. "Early Adolescent Theft," *American Sociological Review*, XXVI (October, 1961), 733-43.

MELVIN A. DUREA. "An Experimental Study of Attitudes Toward Juvenile Delinquency," *Journal of Applied Psychology*, XVII (October, 1933), 522-34.

————. "A Quantitative Method of Diagnosing the Seriousness of Asocial Behavior of Juvenile Delinquents," *Journal of General Psychology*, XIV (April, 1936), 412-20.

MABEL A. ELLIOTT. *Correctional Education and the Delinquent Girl*, Pennsylvania Department of Welfare, Bulletin No. 36 (Harrisburg, Pennsylvania, 1929).

———— and FRANCIS E. MERRILL. *Social Disorganization* (3rd. ed.; New York: Harper and Brothers, 1950).

Essex County Juvenile and Domestic Relations Court. *Problems Presented in the Juvenile and Domestic Relations Court. Annual Report, 1955* (Newark, N.J., 1955).

E. FRANKLIN FRAZIER. *The Negro Family in the United States* (Chicago: University of Chicago Press, 1939).

SHELDON GLUECK and ELEANOR T. GLUECK. *Unraveling Juvenile Delinquency* (New York: The Commonwealth Fund, 1950).

JOHN INKSTER GOODLAD. "Research and Theory Regarding Promotion and Non-Promotion," *Elementary School Journal*, LIII (November, 1952), 150-55.

Selected References

LEO A. GOODMAN. "Ecological Regressions and Behavior of Individuals," *American Sociological Review*, XVIII (December, 1953), 663-64.

HUGH HARTSHORNE and MARK A. MAY, *Studies in Deceit* (New York: The Macmillan Co., 1928).

WILLIAM HEALY. *The Individual Delinquent* (Boston: Little, Brown and Company, 1915).

———— and AUGUSTA BRONNER. "A Comparative Study of Two Groups, Each of 1000 Young Recidivists," *American Journal of Sociology*, XX (July, 1916), 38-52.

———— and ————. *Delinquents and Criminals: Their Making and Unmaking* (New York: The Macmillan Company, 1926).

REUBEN HILL. *Families Under Stress* (New York: Harper and Brothers, 1949).

MARGARET HODGKISS. "The Influence of Broken Homes and Working Mothers," *Smith College Studies in Social Work*, III (March, 1933), 259-74.

JOSEPH A. KAHL and JAMES A. DAVIS. "A Comparison of Indexes of Socio-Economic Status," *American Sociological Review*, XX (June, 1955), 317-25.

WILLIAM C. KVARACEUS. *Juvenile Delinquency and The School* (Yonkers-on-Hudson: World Book Company, 1945).

———— and WALTER B. MILLER. *Delinquent Behavior: Culture and the Individual*, National Education Association of the United States (Washington, D.C., 1959).

KATHERINE F. LENROOT. "Are Broken Homes a Causative Factor in Juvenile Delinquency? II. Discussion," *Social Forces*, X (May, 1932), 527-29.

ELEANOR E. MACCOBY, JOSEPH P. JOHNSON and RUSSELL M. CHURCH. "Community Integration and the Social Control of Juvenile Delinquency," *Journal of Social Issues*, XIV, No. 3 (1958), 38-51.

JULIUS B. MALLER. "Are Broken Homes a Causative Factor in Juvenile Delinquency? IV. Discussion," *Social Forces*, X (May, 1932), 531-33.

GEORGE B. MANGOLD. *Problems of Child Welfare* (rev. ed.; New York: The Macmillan Company, 1924).

WILLIAM MCCORD and JOAN MCCORD, with IRVING KENNETH ZOLA. *Origins of Crime* (New York: Columbia University Press, 1959).

Mercer County Probation Office. *Annual Report, 1957* (Trenton, N.J.), 1958).

THOMAS P. MONAHAN. "Family Status and the Delinquent Child: A Reappraisal and Some New Findings," *Social Forces*, XXXV (March, 1957), 250-58.

W. D. MORRISON. *Juvenile Offenders* (London: T. Fisher Unwin, 1896).

ERNEST R. MOWRER. *Disorganization: Personal and Social* (Philadelphia: J. B. Lippincott Company, 1942).

F. IVAN NYE. "Child Adjustment in Broken and in Unhappy Unbroken Homes," *Marriage and Family Living*, XIX (November, 1957), 356-61.

—————. *Family Relationships and Delinquent Behavior* (New York: John Wiley and Sons, 1958).

HAZEL GRANT ORMSBEE. *The Young Employed Girl* (New York: The Womans Press, 1927).

G. LEWIS PENNER. "An Experiment in Police and Social Agency Cooperation," *The Annals of the American Academy of Political and Social Science*, CCCXXII (March, 1959), 79-88.

HAROLD A. PHELPS. *Contemporary Social Problems* (New York: Prentice-Hall, Inc., 1946).

EDWIN POWERS and HELEN L. WITMER. *An Experiment in the Prevention of Delinquency—The Cambridge-Somerville Youth Study* (New York: Columbia University Press, 1951).

WALTER C. RECKLESS. "A Non Causal Explanation: Containment Theory," *Excerpta Criminologica*, II (March-April, 1962), 131-34.

ALBERT J. REISS, JR. "Delinquency as the Failure of Personal and Social Controls," *American Sociological Review*, XVI (April, 1951), 196-207.

—————. "Unraveling Juvenile Delinquency—An Appraisal of the Research Methods," *American Journal of Sociology*, LVII (September, 1951), 115-120.

Selected References

WILLIAM S. ROBINSON. "Ecological Correlations and the Behavior of Individuals," *American Sociological Review*, XV (June, 1950), 351-57.

SOPHIA M. ROBISON. "The Apparent Effects of the Factors of Race and Nationality on the Registration of Behavior as Delinquent in New York City in 1930," *Publication of the American Sociological Society*, XXVIII (May, 1934), 37-44.

————. *Can Delinquency Be Measured?* (New York: Columbia University Press, 1936).

CARL M. ROSENQUIST. *Social Problems* (New York: Prentice-Hall, Inc., 1940).

SOL RUBIN. "Unraveling Juvenile Delinquency—Illusions in a Research Project," *American Journal of Sociology*, LVII (September, 1951), 107-14.

Russell Sage Foundation. *Boyhood and Lawlessness* (New York, 1914).

ALVIN L. SCHORR. "Mobile Family Living," *Social Casework*, XXXVII (April, 1956), 175-80.

THORSTEN SELLIN. "Race Prejudice in the Administration of Justice," *American Journal of Sociology*, XLI (September, 1935), 212-17.

————. *Culture Conflict and Crime*, Social Science Research Council, Bulletin No. 41 (New York, 1938).

CLIFFORD R. SHAW. *Delinquency Areas*, (Chicago: University of Chicago Press, 1929).

———— and HENRY D. McKAY. "Social Factors in Juvenile Delinquency," National Commission on Law Observance and Enforcement, *Report on the Causes of Crime*, No. 13, II (Washington, 1931).

ERNEST H. SHIDELER. "Family Disintegration and the Delinquent Boy in the United States," *Journal of Criminal Law and Criminology*, VIII (January, 1918), 709-32.

HARRY M. SHULMAN. "Are Broken Homes a Causative Factor in Juvenile Delinquency? III. Discussion," *Social Forces*, X (May, 1932), 529-30.

JOHN SLAWSON. *The Delinquent Boy* (Boston: Richard G. Badger, Publisher, 1926).

PHILIP M. SMITH. "Broken Homes and Delinquency." *Sociology and Social Research*, XXXIX (May, 1955), 307-11.

RICHARD S. STERNE. *Outcome of Parole as Related to Pre-Parole Prognosis*, (Philadelphia: Pennsylvania Committee on Penal Affairs, 1946).

EDWIN H. SUTHERLAND and DONALD R. CRESSEY. *Principles of Criminology* (Philadelphia: J. B. Lippincott Company, 1955).

DONALD R. TAFT. *Criminology* (New York: The Macmillan Company, 1950).

PAUL W. TAPPAN. *Juvenile Delinquency* (New York: The McGraw-Hill Book Company, 1949).

NEGLEY K. TEETERS and JOHN OTTO REINEMANN. *The Challenge of Delinquency* (New York: Prentice-Hall, Inc., 1950).

FREDERIC M. THRASHER. *The Gang* (Chicago: University of Chicago Press, 1927).

JACKSON TOBY. "The Differential Impact of Family Disorganization," *American Sociological Review*, XXII (October, 1957), 505-12.

————. Review of *Family Relationships and Delinquent Behavior*, by F. Ivan Nye (New York: John Wiley and Sons, 1958), in *American Sociological Review*, XXIV (April, 1959), 282-83.

MARTHA BUSHFIELD VANVALEN. "An Approach to Mobile Dependent Families," *Social Casework*, XXXVII (April, 1956), 180-86.

ORVILLE S. WALTERS. "The Religious Background of Fifty Alcoholics," *Quarterly Journal of Studies on Alcohol*, XVIII (September, 1957), 405-16.

WILLIAM W. WATTENBURG. "Delinquency and Only Children, a Study of a 'Category'," *Journal of Abnormal and Social Psychology*, XLIV (July, 1949), 356-66.

————. "Juvenile Repeaters from Two Viewpoints," *American Sociological Review*, XVIII (December, 1953), 631-35.

H. ASHLEY WEEKS. "Male and Female Broken Home Rates by Type of Delinquency," *American Sociological Review*, V (August, 1940), 601-9.

————— and MARGARET G. SMITH. "Juvenile Delinquency and Broken Homes in Spokane, Washington," *Social Forces*, XVIII (October, 1939), 48-55.

JOHN W. M. WHITING, RICHARD KLUCKHOHN and ALBERT ANTHONY. "The Function of Male Initiation Ceremonies at Puberty," *Readings in Social Psychology*, (New York: Holt, Rinehart and Winston, Inc., 1958; Eleanor E. Maccoby, Theodore M. Newcomb and Eugene L. Hartley, eds.), pp. 359-70.

T. J. WOOFTER, JR. "Size of Family in Relation to Family Income and Age of Family Head," *American Sociological Review*, IX (December, 1944), 678-84.

INDEX

(*"t"* following an entry denotes reference to a table)

Index

moving, *see above*, mobility

nativity of delinquent, 33, 122

neighborhood-"bad areas,"
  delinquency rates, 33-37, 39, 64
  results in this study, using wards, 77-80, 79t, 108t; (length of residence, or mobility, and), 79, 83; (immediate or later referral to court and), 79; travel to distant schools and), 34-35, 79-80; (differential law enforcement and), 79-80; (calendar period and), 80
  Census Tracts compared to wards, 123
  changes in areas over time, 123
  interstitial areas, 39
  recreational opportunities, 39

neighborhood-"bad gangs," 39, 80-81, 81t; relation to type of offense, 81, 81t; relation to broken homes, 81; *see also above*, companions in the act

neutral boys, *see above*, mental problems of boy

occupation, of father or head of family, 33, 38-39; head of family unemployed, 37, 71t; of chief wage earner, 70-71, 71t, 109t; U. S. Census classifications, 70

offenses of family members, 86-87; recidivism in family, effect, 87; recent first offenses, 87, 87t; *see also*, Offenses (of listed family members), 109t

only child, *see below*, siblings

paramours, 89t, 125

parents, born abroad (foreign-born parents), 27, 33, 37, 75, 75t, 77, 92, 95, 109t, 122

parents, religions, 50; differing, 27, 74-75, 74t, 77, 92, 95, 110t

physical problems, of boy, 110t, 122; of others, *see above*, disabilities

police policies, change in, 69; *see also above*, court referral

race of offender, 33, 41, 50-51, 65, 119

relief and aid (or social service) to the family, 39, 71-72, 72t, 74, 110t

religion, Protestant faith, 27, 76-77, 95; religious affiliations in general, 76-77, 77t, 92, 110t, 119; conflict, *see above*, parents, religions differing

school retardation, 33, 121

schools, out of neighborhood, 34-35, 79-80

sex of offender, 50-51, 65, 120; female offenders, studies of, 33, 36-37, 44-45, 118, 120

siblings, 85-86; only child, 85-86; 85t, 95; step-siblings, 85, 110t; number of, 85-86, 85t, 109t; ordinal position, 86, 109t; relative position, 86, 110t

social status, 50; *see also above*, occupation of chief wage earner; income, 119

special detriments in broken homes, 88-92

spurious correlations, 71

step-(or foster) parents, 60, 74-75, 88-90, 89t, 110t, 122, 124-25

supervision at home, 27, 50, 63-64, 64t, 66-70, 68t, 77, 92-95, 110t

unemployment, *see above*, occupation; *see also above*, relief and aid

white collar families, *see above*, occupation

working boys (employment of boys), 82, 82t, 109t; age of boy and, 82

Index